Buying the Right RV with Confidence

Second Edition

By

Jim & Loni Macy

BuyingRVBook@gmail.com

Second Edition

ISBN-10: 0-9988218-0-2
ISBN-13: 978-0-9988218-0-1

Preface

It is our goal to help you understand what you are looking at when you walk through an RV. Perhaps, unless you have spent time in the RV of your choice, you may buy the sizzle, but not the steak. Is it perfect? No. Would we do things differently? Yes, with unlimited funds!

We intend to help you understand the practical consequences of what you see. For example, when you look at the kitchen, do you see that beautiful stack of kitchen drawers? Did you open them? Did you count all six? Well, you really can't do much with six drawers if each one is only three or four inches deep! Better to have three drawers that are deep enough to hold the pots, pans, and the utensils you will need.

It is our promise to give you as much of our knowledge, gleaned from our personal experience, and the experience of others in-the-know as we can. This book doesn't address anything about the mechanical operation of engines, transmissions, and the like, but it will help you make that important decision on how to get the RV of your dreams. There are numerous books, blogs, and professional advice articles to help in the areas of mechanics, maintenance, and repair. However, in what to look for and what to avoid in the glitz of an RV, there is as much a lack of information as technical information abounds.

We are not suggesting that you use all the information contained in this short book, or even follow it. An attorney once told us that everything is negotiable, so negotiate. If you want to exchange some of the considerations, at least you will be aware of some of the potential adverse consequences. Call it risk management, not risk aversion. Did we follow all the rules because of what we knew? No! We got what we wanted in spite of not following hard and fast technical information. Did we have the experience to maneuver through the process successfully? Yes, with the help of a good salesman and company! This book contains more than enough information for you to succeed as well.

We hope the information is more than you might want without being overwhelmed, and we leave it to you to prioritize what is important to you.

Dedication

We dedicate this book to those we have learned from along our journey to a more exciting, fulfilling, and adventurous lifestyle. We have made new friends and deepened our relationship with them through the years.

We have gleaned much from friends and acquaintances sitting around the campfire sharing stories, adventures, and preparing for the future through the experience of others. We hope this book will help you too.

Disclaimer

Limits of Liability and Disclaimer of Warranty

Here is the stuff our attorney said we ought to include to make his job easier.

The authors, editors, and publisher of this book and any accompanying materials have used their best efforts in preparing this collectively information. The authors, editors, and publisher, individually or, make no representation or warranties about the accuracy, applicability, fitness, or completeness of the contents of this information. They disclaim any warranties (expressed or implied), merchantability, or fitness for any purpose.

The authors, editors, and publisher shall not be held liable for any loss or other damages, including but not limited to incidental, consequential, or other damages.

The authors, editors, and publisher make no claims for any benefits of the information contained herein.

For more information

Jim or Loni Macy

110 E Center ST. #1035

Madison, SD. 57042

BuyingRVBook@gmail.com

Introduction - Our Story

When we first started to think about living in an RV, we didn't know what we were looking AT when we saw an RV, particularly a Class A motorhome.

Our first foray into purchasing a motorhome lead us to a 1991 31-foot Bounder with a 454 Chevy engine and a Banks Turbo system (We still don't know what the advantage was to the Banks, but apparently it's neat). We bought our first Bounder #1, kept it for four or five years and sold it for $2,700 more than we paid. Not a bad experience.

We learned if you maintain the coach as close to original, then previously owned rigs apparently don't depreciate that much. Of course, if you buy new, then expect to take the financial hit for the privilege of being owner number ONE.

While we had Bounder #1, we purchased Bounder #2. This rig was 36-feet and a diesel pusher with one slide. We had it for a year, traveled the eleven Western states then traded it in for our third motorhome, a 40-foot National RV/Country Coach diesel pusher with two slides. By this time, we had a very solid idea of what we wanted. We had a list of things we wanted, things that were deal-breakers, and things that were negotiable. Once again, by keeping it close to the original, we received a very generous trade-in for Bounder #2.

As we traveled, we found it fun to stop at RV dealerships and browse. We asked questions and walked through hundreds of RVs at dozens of RV lots throughout the Western US. We went to rallies and looked at different models and floorplans; we looked online at the available floorplans. We learned about motorhomes, fifth-wheels, and travel trailers. We still do that, but not with the gusto and anticipation we had in the beginning because we found a high-end motorhome that we thoroughly enjoy and find easy to call home.

Since 2013 we have done RV walk-throughs with acquaintances who are now friends, sharing with them what we've learned and helping them find the right rig.

This book is our way of taking what we have learned over the past years and making it available to anyone wanting to purchase an RV, whether for vacationing or full-time RVing in your very own mobile residency. Whether you are looking for your first, second, or third RV, you will find a golden nugget you can take away from the information contained herein.

We hope this book will help make your purchasing experience less stressful and better equip you to find the rig to fulfill your needs and dreams.

If you have any questions or would like us to help you personally, please feel free to contact us by email.

You may not want to follow or consider certain information or our recommendations and rationale. That's okay. Once we have given you the best information we can, it's your decision. If you had asked us three years ago when we purchased our third motorhome if we considered all the information in this book the answer would be "no," we didn't consciously think about a lot of the information contained in this small micro-tome.

Despite our ignoring some of the information we are offering you, we couldn't be happier with our home or lifestyle. Would we get another RV some day? Possibly, depending on health and change in personal circumstances we may move to a larger unit or downsize to one that is easier to maneuver, park, and maintain.

Table of Contents

CHAPTER 1 / Which is Best for You?

The following is a list of the different types of recreational vehicles available at the time of this writing.

Towables

- Fifth-wheels
  - Toy haulers
- Travel trailers
- Camp trailers
  - A-frame pop-ups trailers
  - Tent trailers
- Teardrops

Motorized

- Class A
  - Bus Conversions
- Class B
  - B+ & Super B
- Class C
  - Super C
- Vans

There is a wide variety of RVs available to complement almost any budget, need, or lifestyle.

Some people like the trailer for its conveniences and advantages, while others prefer the motorhome for its amenities and benefits. Some people like to tow their home with their transportation, and others chose to tow their transportation with their home.

Besides feeling more comfortable pulling a trailer or driving a motorhome, people unconsciously seem to gravitate to one or the other. Once you park your trailer and level it, you have a home base from which to sally forth. But, the same applies to motorhomes unless you aren't towing anything.

People who choose a Class B MH rarely tow. The tradeoff is they are very mobile, but living space is more confined because of the van they are using.

Some use a camp trailer to get to their favorite fishing hole or hunting campsite. Many of the National Parks have size limitations in their campgrounds, so those who want to spend much of their time in the National Park system opt for the shorter and lower height trailers, Class B's or C's.

Insurance premiums may also be a factor in the choice of an RV as are fuel and maintenance expenses. Others will choose one type over another because they have storage space at home for one type of RV but not another.

Trailers are usually easier to store during the winter or for extended periods of time since there is no engine, fuel, or fluids to deteriorate because of disuse. They are easily "winterized."

When you put it all together, most of the components found in a motorhome are the same as those found in a travel trailer or fifth-wheel. It may just come down to intended use, storage, and other non-RV considerations.

Also, circumstances change, so don't feel as though current events tie you into a "forever" choice. What is important is that you are comfortable with your choice at any given time. The RV experience can be less than you hoped for if you are not happy with your choice of rigs. When you look for your RV, consider all your circumstances such as housing, finances, your desire to move around, or to stay in an area for a few months to a year or longer. Many full-timers opt for the fifth-wheel because they only travel two or three times a year, and trailers do better than motorhomes when sitting for months at a time.

Knowing, or at least having an idea, what you want to do with your RV is an important consideration. Ask yourself what you want to accomplish with your purchase and decide which rig will best fit that purpose.

Here are some ideas to consider:

Visiting family and friends	Providing long-term care for someone
Full-time Travel	Hunting or fishing
Sightseeing	Sporting events (NASCAR, football, baseball)
Rallies	Festivals and fairs
Relocating	Traveling to or working in the National Parks system

It's up to you, the world of RVing is exciting, adventurous, and awesome.

Plan what you want to do before you buy your rig. Sure, it will change, but at least you will have a use in mind.

No purpose equals **no goal** equals **no long term interest** and, in the end, you will be unhappy with your purchase and possibly your dreams for the future.

CHAPTER 2 / Towables -The Good & Bad

(There is no ugly)

Let's take a look at some of the Pros and Cons of each towable as well as some reasons owners will pick one over the other.

Fifth-wheels

These are mid to large trailers. They have a kingpin, and the tow vehicle has a plate that locks the king pin into position. With the plate centered over the tow vehicle's rear axle, they are stable when on the road. Toy haulers are designed to have room inside to carry horses, quads, motorcycles, golf carts, or other cargo. This cargo room can be converted into living space if needed.

Pros:

- Large living area. With the trailer width of eight feet and opposing slideouts, there could be up to fifteen and a half feet of living space side to side and as long as the trailer is from the back of the overhang to the rear of the trailer.
- Lighter weight than some of the motorhomes of the same length. Possibly better mileage and easier handling.
- Lower maintenance costs and, if only used occasionally, possibly less in insurance premiums. Many automotive repair shops can maintain the running gear, that is, the brakes, wheel packings, and tires. Many owners service their rig themselves.
- Once parked it can be left as a home base, and the tow vehicle, usually a powerful pickup, can be used for local travel.
- When parked and disconnected the overhang can provide either some patio shelter from the elements or, with the proper curtaining, storage space.
- Seems more "homey" because it lacks the cockpit.

- Usually, an abundance of storage in cupboards and drawers.
- The tow pickup will recharge the trailer batteries when the trailer is being towed or connected with the tow engine running.

Cons:

- Tow vehicle may not get much better mileage when not towing. Consider overall fuel costs.
- Basement or outside storage is usually limited to the area at the beginning of the full height, i.e. not including the overhang. The exception to this storage is when the rear of the trailer also includes very shallow space under a raised floor. Used for things that will lay flat. This rear storage only has a height of six to eight inches, extending from one side of the trailer to the other, and a width (front to back of trailer) of four to six feet.
- The living space is divided between the main floor and the upper floor, and may even have a raised floor at the rear of the rig as well as the front. Elderly fifth-wheel owners have told us, “Anywhere you want to go, you end up climbing stairs.” These trailers may also have more outside steps just to get inside, than most travel trailers.
- With opposing slides drawn in, there is very limited space, perhaps, with access only to the upstairs bedroom and bath, and a small part of the kitchen. We have seen fifth-wheelers with the slides in where even the refrigerator was unavailable. Many fifth-wheels must have at least one slide out to gain access to any more than part of the kitchen and all the living areas except bed and bath.
- Fifth-wheels usually do not have a generator, so they must be plugged into shore power, have solar panels, an external generator, or give up storage space for a built-in generator. This issue becomes more critical in the newer models that have household refrigerators. Some built-in generators run

on propane, and owners have told us that the generator will drink 20 pounds of propane a night. (One gallon of LPG weighs about 4-lbs.).

Who buys fifth-wheels? People that have the tow vehicle and are prepared to pull a large or very large home. They may be full timers, construction workers, or individuals or couples who want to stay in one spot for an extended period of time. These people may not move frequently and want the large living quarters. Some of those we have talked to say they only want to change locations three or four times a year or don't want to pay for the running gear of a motorhome. Some younger families find an economic advantage to owning a fifth-wheel as opposed to a fixed home.

Travel trailers

These are small to large trailers. The smaller trailers can be towed by automobiles and the larger ones by pickup trucks. The connection between the trailer and the tow vehicle is at the back end of the car or truck with a ball hitch. The interior floor of the trailer is all on one level. The iconic trailer might be the aluminum Airstream®, although there are many other models on the roads today.

Pros:

- With the trailer width of eight feet and opposing slide outs there could be up to fifteen and a half feet of living space side to side and as long as the slides on each side. This arrangement makes for a spacious and comfortable living area.
- Lighter weight than some of the towables of the same length, thus offering better mileage and easier handling.
- Lower maintenance costs. Many automotive repair shops can accommodate the running gear, that is, the brakes,

wheel packings, and tires. Many owners service their rig themselves. Better insurance rates may be possible.

- Once parked it may be left as a home base, and the tow vehicle car or pickup can be used for local travel.
- Lower to the ground and lower profile make it easier to enter and exit. The lower profile reduces wind resistance when towing.
- National Parks may be more accessible due to the outside dimensions of the trailer.
- All living space on one level.

Cons:

- Storage space is virtually limited to the inside of the trailer. Any outside storage will be used by the utility connections and equipment. Small bins or storage areas may be accessible from the outside.
- Electric power is limited to the one or two batteries on board. Travel trailers must be plugged into shore power, have solar panels, an external generator, or connected to the tow vehicle's electric system.
- Holding tanks may have smaller capacities (around 30 gals of fresh water) than fifth-wheels. Gray water and black water tanks will be reduced accordingly.

Who buys travel trailers? People who would like all their living space on one level. They also want the advantage of not having to commit their tow vehicle to a new installation of a fifth-wheel plate in the bed of their pickup. Travel trailers are much more adaptable to different tow packages and vehicles. While this may seem like a downgrade from the fifth-wheel, it makes up for a lot by being more flexible in which vehicles can tow them, storage opportunities, and easier parking.

Camp trailers

These are trailers that are designed to get off the beaten path and go camping at the fishing hole, hunting blind, or just get onto some Bureau of Land Management (BLM) areas and dispersed campgrounds.

A-frame pop-ups trailers

The A-frame pop-ups is the name that we have given to the hard-shell collapsible camp trailer made by Aliner® (www.aliner.com) and other manufacturers. The roof line is that of an A-Frame with each half of the roof collapsing for travel and pushing up into the A-Frame for habitation.

Pros:

- Easy to store when not in use.
- Easy to tow. Almost any vehicle from mid-size up to the full-size SUV can tow these trailers. Check with your car's manufacturer to find the hitch weight and the towing weight.
- Good shelter from the elements.
- Has modest kitchen and cooking facilities.

Cons:

- Because of the sloped ceiling, the roof has less room to stand than many other trailers including tent trailers.
- Holding tanks are of limited capacity and must be frequently dumped. A Porta Pottie® may be the only toilet facility short of campground restrooms.

Tent trailers

These are the low profile trailers that open into a large living area in the middle of the trailer. They usually have one or two canvas sleeping locations that pull out from the front and back as well as fold-out canvas sides for more interior space.

Pros:

- A low travel profile makes it easy to tow. Many are low enough that the interior tow vehicle mirror can see over the top of the trailer.
- Maneuverable and able to get into those favorite fishing or hunting spots Sleeps several people with two beds, one at each end of the rig.

Cons:

- Canvas sleeping areas are more fragile than hard sides.
- Little protection from outside temperatures due to little insulation.
- Some of these units may have furnaces and air conditioning.
- Those with air conditioning need an aftermarket generator to produce power.
- Limited kitchen/cooking, and toileting areas.

Who buys camping trailers? Campers who want to get away from the work-a-day world and enjoy nature and be more comfortable than sleeping in a tent or on the ground.

These trailers can also serve as a base camp for hikers, climbers, hunters, and fishermen. Camping trailers are an entry level for many people to explore the idea of vacationing in their own trailer. Camping trailers lend to the authentic camping experience, with the family or fellow sportsmen.

Teardrops

These iconic trailers harken back to the early travel in automobiles. The teardrops are small enough to be towed by almost any auto and provide sleeping shelter from the elements.

Many of the newer ones are equipped with LED lighting and also have modern TVs that use less electricity. The back end or trunk lid opens to a modest kitchen with a few gallons of water, small wash basin, and a one or two burner propane or white gas stove.

It usually includes a small ice box for perishables.

Pros:

- Can be towed by almost any vehicle.
- They are iconic and attract lots of attention.
- They are nostalgic and fun to use for short vacations and get togethers.
- Designed for one or two people or a person and a fur baby.

Cons:

- Not much storage space. Use the back of your car or tow vehicle as the storage solution.
- Cramped quarters. Sitting up in bed or laying down are your only options since the entire interior is the bed.
- Unless equipped with an awning or an outside attached shelter the door opens to the outside directly from the bed.
- Dressing can be an issue.
- Without some add-on shelter keeping the bed dry during inclement weather is also a problem.

Who buys these teardrops? People who want to have fun, enjoy the attention, and associate with other teardrop owners. Some owners rehabilitate the older models or build new ones using

DIY kits. It's all about the teardrop and having one to play with and stay in for short periods of time.

CHAPTER 3 / Motorized -The Good & Bad

(No ugly here either)

While the motorized designations are Class "A," "B," or "C" these classifications have nothing to do with a grade indicating which is better, bigger, or more prestigious.

Class A

This type of motorhome resembles a bus. In fact, some Class A's are converted from passenger buses into a motorhome with living space. Unless a newer model, conversions do not have slides. The Class A interior and cockpit sit higher than most of the traffic around it. They may have an entrance door in the front or mid-ship somewhere along the curbside of the vehicle.

Pros:

- Living space and home all in one unit. Large enough to tow your sightseeing vehicle or wheeled toys.
- Your towed vehicle is usually more economical to drive than the usual pickups that tow fifth-wheels.
- Able to access all your home without stopping. Passengers can get to the kitchen for a snack or use the toilet facilities without the need to stop.
- No need to exit the vehicle to set it up for an overnight stop. Especially handy in inclement weather.
- Can be used with the slides in or out.
- Coach is leveled by three or four jacks capable of raising and holding the rig level, even with wheels off the ground.

Hydraulic jacks can accommodate around ten inches of difference in level front to rear.

- Some, especially the conversions and newer diesel rigs use airbags to level. Owners have told us the air bags can level about a five-inch difference in level front to back.
- Diesel pushers have the engine in the rear which makes for a quieter ride than an engine at the front.
- Storage can be plentiful depending on the style of the basement.
- Regular maintenance may be less frequent than for smaller vehicles.

Cons:

- Many consider the maintenance much more expensive than either the pickups or other tow vehicles.
- Insurance may be more than trailers, especially if the Class A is used infrequently.
- Some state laws target motorhomes for size and number of axles. A “CDL” may be required.
- On a foot-by-foot basis, most MHs are heavier than trailers. A 40-foot motorhome can have a gross vehicle weight (GVW) of 40,000 lbs. or more, while a similar length trailer may weigh in at 26,000 pounds.
- Service and repairs are mostly limited to mobile repairs, truck stops and truck repair companies.
- The large interior space may make it harder to heat or cool. Open windows can help move air through the interior. Awnings can provide some shade. And, finally, two or three air conditioners may help cool the interior when shore power is available. Most A/C units also act as heat pumps but are an expensive way to heat with the onboard generator.
- Because of their size, two components are necessary to consider. First is the wheelbase and second is the tail overhang. We will discuss these issues later on, with other safety and driving issues.

- With nothing in front of the driver and navigator's chairs, Captain's chairs, the danger involved in front end collision and collateral damage to the occupants is another safety factor.
- Driving must be defensive at the foremost. Just because you are driving a big vehicle does not necessarily mean you are safe. Look for the chapter on driving.

Who buys the Class A? People who want all the comforts of home in one vehicle and still be able to travel.

Class B including B+ and Super B's

Here is one of the toughest rigs to describe. Class B's are sometimes referred to as camper vans. Some consider this class to be the smallest of the RV's.

Class B's are similar to vans, but in most cases more versatile. The body may flare out on both sides of the cabin area. Name brands include Roadtrek®, Pleasure Way®, and others. These smaller RVs are easy to drive, park, and are economical to operate. A large rental market using Class B is being addressed by Juicy®, Escape®, and others. The B+ and Super B may be difficult to distinguish from the class C's because they may have a loft over the cabin. The loft may be sculpted into the body and look very sleek and aerodynamic.

Pros:

- Built on a Ford, Chevy, or Mercedes chassis with an engine to power the body and contents.
- Usually, around twenty to twenty-two feet in length, lending itself to easy parking and maneuvering through a town or parking lot.

- No need to tow a sightseeing vehicle since the mileage and maneuverability are consistent with what you might tow. Usually, the learning curve to drive one of these RVs is quick and easy since they are pretty much like your family car or SUV.
- All the comforts of home with shower, head (or Porta Potty®), kitchen, and sleeping areas. The livingroom area may have a horseshoe-shaped couch or seating that converts into a full sized bed.
- With the engine out front, you have a vehicle that is inherently safer than a rear engine vehicle. But then, thousands of VW buses have been around for decades!

Cons:

- Storage space is limited.
- The bed is wall to wall so that you won't roll out of bed, but it can be a problem to make. Think sleeping bag rather than sheets and blankets.
- Cannot use the seating area as such if the bed isn't disassembled. The cushions rearranged to be the back of the seats and the foot-well cleared of any bed supports.
- If camping in a campground it may be difficult to hold a campsite while away sightseeing, or other activities.
- Part of the common area inside may be used for bathing space, thus limiting inside movement during shower time.
- Toilet facilities, shower, and basin all use the same space accommodating one person at a time.
- Limited holding tanks. Holding tanks may allow for one shower before needing to empty the grey tank or fill fresh tank.

The Super B and the B+ are larger and offer more storage, sleeping, and general use areas. It is these B's which are difficult in determining if the unit is a B or C. These larger B's are built on a heavier duty frame and have a beefed up engine. They may also include slides, which expand the interior exponentially.

Because of the expanded size, you may have to take more driving time than a smaller B to learn the vehicle's driving limitations. The reward will be to enjoy the more expansive interior room.

Who buys the B or B+? Many people downsize because of health or family reasons. Some will downsize, and put a small travel trailer behind the B, so the tow vehicle also becomes the sightseeing vehicle. Ingenious! Two sleeping areas, two dining areas, two bathing areas, and a trailer to hold a campsite for a few days while sightseeing overnight in the B. Other people buy the B to sightsee on an occasional basis, attend 4-H and other shows, sporting events, rallies, or convoy with others of a like mind.

Class C including Super C's

These rigs are built on a truck frame and have a loft over the truck's cab. A Class C RV is typically built on a van or truck chassis, with an attached cab and sleeping area in the loft area over the cab. C's can be from around 23 to 33 feet in length and will include a small dining area, living area seating, kitchen, and bathroom. Some models also feature one or more slide-outs and a separate rear bedroom, and some may have sleeping arrangements for up to nine people.

Where the class B flairs from cab out on either side, there is usually a sharp demarcation of the wider living area in a C. The living quarters extend out from the cab to a nominal width of eight feet. They will have doors to the cab on both the passenger's and driver's sides as well as a door entering the living area. Newer C class may have slides depending on the manufacturer.

The smaller C's may depend on leveling blocks, once placed on the ground the rig is driven onto the blocks for leveling. Some of the larger units and the Super C's have leveling jacks that can compensate for many inches in site slope.

Pros:

- Cab and engines are much like pickup trucks.
- The Super C's are usually built on a Freightliner truck chassis.
- Engine out front.
- Tow vehicle optional depending on the size of the rig.
- These coaches bridge the gap between the class A and B model. They have features of both other classes from cab structure to spacious living quarters.
- Towing a utility trailer with motorcycles or quads is possible
- Towing a boat or another vehicle is possible and lends itself to a more diverse experience.

Cons:

- If the rig is small, then many of the disadvantages that apply to the B class may apply to the C class.. For example, the bed in the loft area may be wall to wall or have walls on three sides. Larger units may have separate sleeping areas.
- Leveling may be difficult especially in inclement weather or soft dirt at the site.
- If camping in a campground it may be difficult to hold a campsite while away sightseeing, or other away activities.

Who buys C's and super C's? People who like the opulence of the full sized motorhome and the safety of the engine in front of the occupants. Retired truck drivers may be the largest segment of Super C owners. Others who have purchased C's in the past and liked the feel of the C may upgrade to the Super C.

Vans

This group is similar to the class B. There is no change in width from front to back. Van configurations may include a raised roof or a pop-up roof and may have a sliding door or "barn doors" opening on one or both sides for access to the living area. They may also have barn doors at the rear or a hatch that opens upwards.

Van conversions are almost self-explanatory because these RV's are essentially vans otherwise used for commercial purposes. Owners or commercial companies, convert these RVs, by outfitting the interiors for living quarters as an RV.

Pros:

- Easy on the pocketbook
- Great way to try out RVing. Do you want the outdoor adventure with the indoor protection from weather and the elements, weekend excursions, rallies and sporting events, or fishing or hunting shelter? Go camping for a weekend or a week in a rental.
- Used mostly for rentals, but it gives you a way to check out what you like and what you don't like. Don't be afraid to rent the class you think you might want to purchase.
- Excellent for going from one campground with hookups or bathing facilities to the next campground.

Cons:

- Small space designed for short term use, camping and overnight adventures, even if you use it for a week or two. With planning, you will weed out all the unnecessary stuff.
- The bed isn't very forgiving but possibly better than an air mattress and a tent.
- Very limited ability to be self-contained for more than a few days.

- Limited holding tanks and bathing opportunities.
- Little storage, including what may be under a false floor and accessible from the side doors.
- Seating in the living area doubles as the bed by rearranging the cushions.
- Kitchen and cooking area is accessed at the back of the vehicle by opening the rear doors or hatch. Small stove using propane bottles.
- No long-term use as a self-contained vehicle.
- No onboard toilet facilities, possible portable toilets are the exception.
- Offers little protection from extreme heat or cold.
- The cooking area may be exposed to the weather.
- When cooking the living area is open to the outside temperature.

Who buys vans? Some who want a smaller RV or use the vehicle infrequently for camping. Many companies are utilizing this class for tourist and rental vehicles.

Whatever you think you might want your RV to do for you try it out. Do you want the outdoor adventure with the indoor protection from weather and the elements, weekend excursions, rallies and sporting events, or fishing or hunting shelter? Whether class A, B, C and C+, or trailers, spend the money and the time to get to know what you want.

CHAPTER 4 / Other Comparisons

Now that we have described the various types of towables and motorized RV's we can take a look at some of the other considerations that flow across the different types of RV's.

Hitches generally fall into three classifications, kingpin, extendable hitches, and ridged ball hitches. Each group has a primary purpose, and in the case of the rigid and extendable hitches there may be some crossover.

Kingpin hitches can be pulled, backed up, and are generally user-friendly. They are used for towing heavier trailers, and it is the hitch all eighteen wheelers use.

Ball hitches, fall into the rigid hitch classification, whether for a towed vehicle or trailer. These hitches are made from a rigid triangular frame with a ball receiver at the apex. With this type of hitch, you will be able to backup and maneuver in reverse. These hitches typically pull a travel or camping trailer and the hitch is attached to what is being towed. Except for Jeeps, ridged hitches are rarely attached to autos.

Extendable hitches such as the Blue Ox® and the Falcon series by Roadmaster® along with the foldable ball hitches belong to the second classification. According to the manufacturers, they cannot be backed without a high potential for damage to the hitch mechanism, and the companies don't warranty the product if it was damaged while backing. Sure, there is the exception to damaging the towbar while backing. We have talked to people who have backed more than 100 or so feet with a tow car attached. Others were not so fortunate and ruined their tow bar by backing only a few feet. Manufacturers of extendable hitches advise against backing with this type of hitch even a few inches. While this style hitch is much easier to hook up and disengage the towed vehicle, they are designed only to pull, not push. Back-upper beware!

Beyond hitches, interior components such as appliances, furniture, and plumbing fixtures for fifth-wheels, travel trailers, and virtually all motorhomes are supplied by a few manufacturers. The exception is in the newer RVs where you may find residential refrigerators, and upgraded sinks, and basins.

Leveling systems and slide extenders are provided by three companies. They are, HWH and Power Gear. Both of these companies provide leveling systems and slide extenders. The third is Accu-Slide BAL®, which moves slides by way of a cable system. We have had both HGH and Power Gear on our rigs, and it is a toss-up which is better. Personal preference is with HGH, but there is nothing but a gut reaction for our preference. Maybe it is just the name.

RV refrigerators for the larger and older motorhomes and travel trailers may be limited to Dometic® or Norcold®. You may also see Coleman® in the smaller rigs. The newer and larger models of fifth-wheels and Class A motorhomes may have residential refrigerators installed.

RV refrigerators cool with a small flame or electric heat source and ammonia. The residential refrigerators must be run on 120V AC for the compressor to function.

People we've talked to seem to like the residential refers. Some have told us that they had to learn how to pack the shelves for travel in a way that kept the contents from tipping over or sliding around, but all in all the response has been more positive than not.

- **Recommendation:** We prefer to stick with the tried and true RV refrigerators.

- **Rationale:** Residential refrigerators were made to stay at home. Given the cost of repair or replacement and the fact that the newer models are designed to run continuously, a reliable power source is necessary. Residential refrigerators may need repair or replacement in three to seven years.

Water heaters may be propane or a combination of propane or, electric. Some water heaters have an anode to prevent corrosion. This anode needs to be replaced on a regular basis. We have found that, for us, once a year is okay, but you should check with the manufacturer's recommendations. A modern water heating system is the Aqua-Hot® system. The larger model can heat your water and the floor of your rig. Newer rigs may have an instant hot water delivery system. Aftermarket instant systems are built to slide into the older water heater space without space modification.

Inverters change 12-volt electricity into 110-120-volt alternating (household) current. There are a few manufacturers, and we have found the Xantrex® inverter system to be user-friendly. Yes, there are others smaller and larger. Be sure the inverter you have is adequate for the demands of your maximum electrical needs. The inverter is an issue that a dealer or the manufacturer can advise what is best for you.

Solar panels and controllers can be another valuable source of electric power. Because of the rapid developments in this industry, we do not have the experience to advise you on a particular product. That said, owners we have talked to think very highly of their solar systems, and some told us the panels cut their generator usage by 75% or more. Solar panels may be a positive addition unless you plan on spending most or all your time using shore-power, i.e., in a campground or facility where you can tap into the outside power source.

Wheels, tires, and axle information is not intended to be too technical; but it is important to consider. Larger motorhomes will have either 19.5 or 22.5-inch wheels. The 22.5-inch rims are the same as most trucks. These bigger tires are more expensive but will have enough tread to go 150,000 miles or so. More important is the age of the tire. Most RV manufacturers recommend replacing the tires every four years.

Tire failure begins with oxidation and sun damage to the tires when they are sitting still. A tire that is sitting still is a rotting tire. A rolling tire is a happy tire because the oils can move throughout the rubber keeping it more flexible and lubricated. If you look at a tire, you can check the age after the DOT stamp. Since 2000, the four numbers after the DOT will tell you the week of manufacture. For example 23 = the 23rd week of the year and the last two numbers the year of manufacture, e.g., 16 = 2016. So a DOT with the number 2316 indicates the twenty-third week of 2016. You want a young new tire. If the stamp said 0814, you would be looking at a tire that had been sitting in a warehouse since February of 2014. By 2016, half the recommended useful life of the tire is gone before you buy it.

Fifth-wheels and travel trailers use smaller tires more like an automobile or small truck tires. The same tire information holds true for towables. If your trailer, fifth-wheel or camp trailer sits for extended times, tire safety ought to be a top priority before moving.

Axles are the next weight bearing consideration. While the tires carry the weight on the road, axles divide that weight into manageable chunks. The more axles, the less weight each carries. The more axles, the more tire scrubbing because only one axle can track what the front wheels are doing. The others scrape sideways on tight turns. If the turn is a gentle one, then scrubbing isn't an issue, but on curvy roads, right angle turns, backing into or turning out of a campsite, or making a U-turn scrubbing can decrease the life of the tire tread.

Some motorhomes have a tag axle. A tag axle is one that doesn't do anything except carry weight. It doesn't steer; it doesn't drive; it simply carries weight. You may see these axles on the larger 40+ foot MHs or some older models such as the classic Cortez MH. Here is a problem. Some states require you to have a commercial driver's license to drive a three-axle vehicle. A CDL requires you to pass a physical every two years. If you don't pass the medical exam, you don't have a valid CDL.

The length of the RV can be an issue for other reasons. Many RV resorts and parks cannot accommodate larger rigs. Camping sites for a fifth-wheel, travel trailer or motorhome exceeding 36 feet may not be available or allowed. Many of the National Parks cannot accommodate larger rigs. Some states restrict the travel of 45-foot rigs to state highways or freeways except for fuel, repairs, or food.

Our preference when we purchased our motorhome was to have only two axles and no more than 40-feet in length. Our thought was that since our driver's licenses were issued in California, we would limit ourselves to what we could legally drive without a CDL or Class A license. We found the MH that was for us, and we have encountered no problems.

Other states usually reciprocate by allowing drivers licensed in less restrictive states to travel without issue through the more restrictive states. For example, if your driver's license is from South Dakota, you could drive any length motorhome and pull two trailers.

Another consideration is whether the rig is powered by a diesel or gasoline engine. In a Class A motorhome, the gasoline engine will be at the front of the coach and the diesel at the rear. The gas motor will have a "dog house," a raised floor which encloses the engine compartment. This covering can be from a few inches to a foot or more in height. Engine noise may be significant and can make communication difficult. Super C's have the motor out front, and many retired truck drivers want to hear the engine, and they feel an out-front engine gives a margin of safety. Class A diesel pusher motorhomes have the engine at the rear. There is less engine noise and more cargo space below because there is no drive train running down the middle of the chassis.

By the way, diesel engines and the chassis that carry them add a significant dollar value to the coach. A diesel engine could add as much as $30,000 to $60,000 or more to the cost of a motorhome. Today many manufacturers are building coaches with gasoline engines as a cost cutting feature.

- **Recommendation**: It all depends on the state where you hold your driver's license. Your state's limitations will determine what you can buy without getting a Commercial Driver's License.

- **Rationale**: Save yourself legal issues before you buy and know what steps you want to take if your state requires a CDL. Your choices would be to establish a domicile in a different state or get a CDL license. One solution may not be any more complicated than the other.

CHAPTER 5 / What About Weight?

You will run into terms that describe the weight limits of either a motorized vehicle, a trailer, fifth-wheel, or combined vehicle weight rating. Please note that the weight ratings are for the vehicle as supplied by the manufacturer with all necessary fluids. It does not include after-market installations or dealer added equipment.

These terms and weight explanations are relevant and have a great deal to do with loading and driving your new rig safely. If you are overweight, it affects your stopping time. If you are heavy on the front, you may have steering issues. If your rig is unbalanced side to side, you may lose control of your rig. The weight and weight distribution will also affect tire and axle wear.

By being aware before you buy, you may avoid safety issues and have an easier time of driving your new rig.

Curb Weight (CW) is the vehicle's weight, including necessary fluids and lubricants as well as equipment installed by the factory. It does not include people, personal contents, dealer or aftermarket equipment installations.

Gross Vehicle Weight (GVW) is the curb weight plus **people**, contents, dealer or an aftermarket equipment installation. GVW is just the weight of your vehicle at a point in time. If a trailer is attached, add the tongue weight to the GVW.

Gross Vehicle Weight Rating (GVWR) is the most weight the vehicle was built to bear.

Gross Axle Weight Rating (GAWR) is the greatest load capacity for each axle component. This rating includes tires, suspension components, and axle. Usually, the rear axle has a higher GAWR than the front. Adding the axles' weight ratings together will **not** give you the gross vehicle weight rating. The GVWR will almost always be lower than the sum of the axle load ratings added together. You will want to know what the axles can carry, and you need to know how the weight is distributed on each axle. By weighing each set of wheels on the axle, you will recognize if you are balanced from side to side and front to back.

All this may seem overwhelming right now, but as you look at rigs, whether a trailer or motorized, you will begin to make sense of these figures and what they mean. How much weight you can load is found by subtracting the **Curb Weight** from the **Gross Vehicle Weight Rating**.

Many manufacturers build their rigs close to rating maximums. You may find that the cargo weight, including passengers, is less than one thousand pounds. Consider your fresh water holding tank of 100 gallons. At eight pounds per gallon, you have less than two hundred pounds of additional cargo. Two occupants weighing an average of one hundred pounds each has just topped out your carrying capacity. In this scenario, your choices are to empty the fresh water, partially empty it, or be overweight.

The following weight definitions apply to vehicles being towed and will be important to those opting for trailers and fifth-wheels. Towing a car with a motorhome is usually less critical and can be addressed by the motorhome manufacturer and the automobile manufacturer,

Unloaded Vehicle Weight Rating is the weight of the trailer including required fluids and any equipment usually installed at the factory. It does not include people, personal contents, or aftermarket equipment installed by a dealer.

Gross Trailer **Weight (GTW)** is the weight of a fully loaded trailer. By knowing your GTW, you know how much stuff you can load into your trailer. Subtract the UVWR from the GTW, and you will have a good idea how much you can put in your trailer.

Gross Combined Weight Rating (GCWR) is the greatest combined weight of the towing vehicle (including things & people) and the trailer (including all the stuff in it). Just subtract the UVWR from the GTW to know how much you can load into your trailer.

The tongue weights are pretty much self-explanatory in that they refer to the downward weight on the hitch. It might be interesting to note that an unloaded trailer may have a greater tongue weight than a loaded trailer if the load in the trailer is balanced so that more weight is behind the trailer axle than in front. In any case, follow the tongue weight as given.

And, the final weight definition you ought to know about if you are towing.

Maximum Trailer Weight (MTW) is the maximum weight that another vehicle may tow. This weight will vary from one tow vehicle to another. You can quickly calculate the MTW for your vehicle. Subtract the weight of the loaded trailer, GTW, from the Gross Combined Weight Rating. By way of illustration, assume the GCWR is 30,000 pounds, the towing vehicle with passengers is 4,000 lbs. Therefore the maximum trailer weight would be 30,000 minus 4,000 or 26,000 pounds.

Whew! These numbers are important, but may not seem so right now. But be aware of them and ask questions before you buy. Be sure to ask if you are asking the right questions so you will be informed of all you need to know, even if you don't know what to ask. You need to know how much stuff you can safely put in your motorhome or trailer. Take the time and decide whether or not you need a lighter weight trailer or motorhome or maybe you need a larger one with more cargo capacity.

Now, the only question is whether or not your tow vehicle has the power to pull your trailer. That question can be answered by the auto (truck) manufacturer. We have seen trailers so small you only have room to sleep, all because the car was not rated for towing anything more than a thousand pounds. Find your towed before you look for your tow vehicle.

The next obstacle to conquer is to estimate the weight of all the stuff you want to take with you.

Are you considering full-time living in your RV? If so, honing down your possessions to what you need and want to take with you is more critical than if you are going to travel for a week or two or even a few months while vacationing. On vacation, you can always leave goodies behind to come home to at the end of your journey. You can pretty well estimate the weight of food, clothing, and essentials by hefting them and noting on paper your estimates. You can also start with weights you know. For instance, you know for sure that a 40lb. bag of dog food weighs 40lbs. Another given is your weight, the weight of water, 8 pounds per gallon. Entertainment, e.g., books, DVDs, yes, they weigh something, computers and electronics, and a myriad of other items that may be indispensable. The Appendix at the end of the book may help in your pursuit of weighing in on how much things weigh.

Again, if you do the tedious heavy lifting before you begin your search in earnest, you will go into your adventure well armed to find the right coach or trailer for you. Your informed decision now will make for a safer journey when you hit the road. Please take your time, sit down, dream, plan, and set your sights in the right direction.

Same stuff - different names

RVIA weight labels

The Recreation Vehicle Industry Association (RVIA) set requirements for RV manufacturer members to reveal the weight information so buyers and owners could better understand and comply with the weight limitations of their motorhomes. After the implementation of these standards in 1996, the following labels are found on a label somewhere in the coach. Look in cabinets including the bathroom. Many of these newer stickers impart the same information as those described above but may be more understandable for those not accustomed to label meanings. For the most part, this section is simply a restatement of the information we just covered, but with a new and more exciting name.

The Unloaded Vehicle Weight (UVW) is simply the weight of the motorhome as built at the factory with full fuel, engine oil, and coolants. This label is same as the **Curb Weight** previously listed

.

Sleeping Capacity Weight Rating (SCWR) is the weight that manufacturer has designated as the number of sleeping places multiplied by 154 pounds or 70 kilograms. (Now you know why some manufacturers will build a trailer to sleep eight or more people).

The Net Carrying Capacity (NCC) is the maximum weight of all occupants **including** the driver and all cargo, e.g. dealer-installed accessories, the tongue weight of the towed vehicle, LP gas, tools, food, fresh water, personal belongings, and clothing. Recently this label has been dropped from the new RVIA calculations.

Cargo Carrying Capacity (CCC) is the **GVWR** minus each of the following: UVW, full fresh water weight, including water-heater - approximately 8 pounds per gal, the weight of full LP-gas, about 4 lbs. per gal, and **SCWR**.

Based on personal calculations of:

Real passengers carried with their maximum weight,

The amount of fresh water onboard (8 Lbs./Gal),

And the quantity of LP-gas on board (tanks are measured by how many pounds of gas they hold – 4lbs/gal).

Maybe this labeling can make it easier to figure the cargo carrying capacity. But maybe not!

- **Recommendation**: Have your new rig weighed by one of the RV clubs that uses individual wheel scales or at a truck stop where you will get an axle-by-axle weight.

- **Rationale**: We are not aware of any laws requiring you to stop at weigh stations. However, some states may require it if: 1) your motorized vehicle has more than two axles or 2) is more than 40 feet long.

CHAPTER 6 / Deal(er) no Deal(er)

Hopefully, the rest of this book will be more exciting than the previous "classroom" study, which is always the most tedious part of finding your new RV.

Armed with the information we have shared so far, you can make up a list of your wants. Forget the sizzle. You are looking for the steak.

Size does matter and it appears that when you add 6-feet in length, the difference is in the middle. That is, the living, dining and kitchen areas are the ones that become roomier.

Take a look online at the floor plans offered by different manufacturers. Soon you will realize that many of the features are the same from manufacturer to manufacturer and across the trailer, fifth-wheel, and motorhome styles.

How large a rig and what carrying capacity do you want?

Do you want a trailer or motorhome?

You will need to sit in and spend some time in those that made the first cut. Possibly you will want to rent the style of your choice.

Do you look at rigs or coaches on the dealer's lot or do you look online for individuals selling RVs?

Dealers have more to show you all in one place. They don't have to sell you a rig right now, and if someone buys the one you thought you wanted, there will be other purchase options later on.

Dealers have better access to financing and giving you the facts about the value and about features and benefits. You can check online with the NADA RV price guide. Talk to the salesperson, let him or her know what you are looking for, your financial requirements and situation, and your time-frame to buy. They can lead you in the right direction. Many dealers have access to RVs across the country, so you are not limited to what is in front of you. Remember the first few forays into the RV world will help you in your learning process.

It will be up to you to turn on your BS radar and be sure it is properly engaged.

Is the salesperson interested in you because he wants to help in your education or is he just wanting to make a deal? Some RV dealers are there to hustle you into a purchase that may not be right for you. If you detect that mentality, then leave! It's your wallet! You need to stay in charge and make decisions based on reliable information.

Your first decision is whether you feel good with the salesperson. Second is whether or not you feel you can trust the company. In our experience of visiting a hundred or more RV lots throughout the twelve Western states, most dealers are willing to help and willing to give honest answers. But, there is always the exception, so buyer beware. Most RV sales are considerably larger than the average auto sale. Hence, there is more of a need to establish trust on both sides. Your confidence in the seller ought to be as great as or greater than your fear of a poor investment.

Individuals selling their personal rigs is another story. It has been our experience that many of the non-dealer sales may be too good to be true. We have talked to private parties, and we feel more confident that the dealer will be better equipped to give you useful information. Too many times the private party seller is simply uninformed.

Private owners seem to be more anxious to make the sale than the dealers and may not disclose all the issues with their coach. This rule isn't always true, but you must be alert for the overzealous selling in the private sale arena. Also be aware that the seller doesn't necessarily know what he or she is selling.

Personally, our choice would be the reputable dealer. With either dealer or individual sales, spend the extra money to have the rig of your choice inspected by a certified inspector. It may cost you up to $1000 or more to have a qualified inspection done on a Class A but it could save you many times that in unforeseen expenses later on.

A good dealer will also give you a walk through and explain how each component works. If you or the dealer finds something isn't functioning correctly, the dealer has the service shop to address any issue you have found. Not so with an individual seller.

In addition to the issues we just enumerated, dealers can help with financing and insurance which is much different than car insurance. Finally, dealers are more likely to stand behind the sale than an individual. After all, they don't want to sell you a vehicle that will cause you problems and heartache right away. Their referral reputation is at stake. Dealers may also offer things you need but don't yet know you need. Some dealers we have met will include a driving course at no additional cost when you buy from them. The individual probably doesn't care about any follow-up as soon as your check clears the bank. He has nothing to lose, the dealer does. In the end, it is up to you.

- **Recommendation**: Get an extended warranty on your RV. Some warranty companies will absorb the cost of the inspection for their protection as well as yours. If your rig is new add the extended warranty as the manufacturer's warranty is expiring. If you're getting a used rig check with various companies to find the age that they will cover. Evaluate cost vs. coverage.

- **Rationale**: Repairs will be expensive and the coverage may well be worth the premium, especially on older rigs. In any event you will want a deep pocket to take care of those repairs you don't make yourself.

CHAPTER 7 / Steak or Sizzle?

You may feel overwhelmed by what you have already learned, but when investing somewhere from $40,000 to $250,000 or more, you might as well indulge yourself in getting it right. Spend adequate time with the details.

What is steak and what is sizzle? It's our opinion that the interior designers of the more expensive RVs have probably never used, travelled, or slept in an RV. They may have cut photos out of Home and Garden or House Beautiful and then used the photos to make the motorhomes more glamorous. A manufacturer told us that we could have anything we wanted as long as we kept throwing money at it.

While that may be true, few of us have that luxury. There is a limit to the funds we can invest in our RV, and we have to make some concessions as to interior and exterior design. Remember that all the fixtures that comprise the inside components or appliances in your RV are found in virtually every other coach or trailer.

Sizzle	Steak
The mirror on the ceiling in the livingroom.	Cleaning the mirror. Getting that thin coating of kitchen grease removed.
The rope mood-lighting around the mirror on the ceiling.	Working around or replacing the rope lighting
A washer-dryer combination or dishwasher in the coach.	Only usable when connected to shore power, water, and sewer.
Lovely colors and decorating ideas	Solid cabinet and wall construction. Practical or Pretty?
Beautiful window dressings	Do the window treatments allow airflow when in use while giving you the privacy you want?
Mirrors in every room -They make rooms look spacious	Consider cleaning mirrors
A rich dark-wood interior	Having to have the lights on so the dimly lighted interior doesn't become cave-like
Lamps, vases, or personal touchs	Use museum putty or remove for travel

When you look at the RV of your dreams, you see the sizzle and the steak. Once you are aware of the "Steak", you can make decisions based on what you know, not just on the sizzle. Don't be discouraged if you like the mood lighting, mirrors, and all the glamorous add-ons. Just be aware that there is a steak side to what you see.

If you want it, get it!

CHAPTER 8 / The Exterior Walkthrough

By now you should know what you are looking for regarding onboard storage space and the weight requirements that meet your lifestyle. You ought to be pretty sure if you want a diesel or gas engine, van, travel trailer, fifth-wheel, or a Class B, C, or A MH.

We will divide the walkthrough into two distinct activities and point things out as we look at an imaginary rig. Many of the items we mention will apply from one class to another and even from the motorized to the travel trailer and fifth-wheel.

We will begin with an imaginary walk through a Class A motorhome. Some of the items will not be available on other models simply because there may not be enough space for the manufacturer to include everything in the smaller rigs.

First, the outside, probably of more interest to the drivers (pilot), and second the inside living, possibly of more concern to the navigators (co-pilots). We will point out things that we have found valuable to both ourselves and other owners. We will give you our reasoning so you can determine if it is important to you. Starting at the front curbside corner of the rig and moving around in a clockwise direction. Here we go!

Mirror placement may be set in front of the rig, or to the side, much like an automobile's side mirrors. They may have the driver's side mirror as a car's would be, and the passenger side in front of the forward most part of the RV. We prefer both mirrors to be in front of the windshield. Beyond that, we like the mirrors to be suspended from the top rather than supported from below.

- **Recommendation**: Our first choice would be mirrors top suspended and with both in front of the windshield. Next would be mirrors mounted from below but still with both in front of the windshield. The least acceptable would be having one or both mirrors mounted to the side of the rig.

- **Rationale**: Side mirrors such as those found on cars may be unusable at certain times of the day, dependent on your direction of travel. We have found that mirrors to the side tend to reflect light from the dashboard back and forth, so it is virtually impossible to see what is behind you in one or both mirrors. Front mounted mirrors have nothing to reflect side to side, so are usable unless the sun is to your rear at a low angle. Also, the driver can see what is in the mirror without turning his or her head so far to the left or right. Suspended mirrors have less of a chance of obscuring a pet, person, or car in the blind spot created by the mirror. Believe it or not, a mirror can hide a full grown person standing behind it.

Entry doors may be located at the front or mid-ship of the RV. Make sure the entry door is wide enough to pass through easily, even with bags of groceries or laundry. If the door is too narrow, you may find it aggravating to use on a daily basis. Also, you might want to count the steps and notice how the steps retract. Check the retracting steps for sagging by standing on each one. Do they sag and tip down at the leading edge or one side or the other? If they do, they will need to be repaired or replaced.

Trailer steps usually fold up and extend by pulling or pushing by hand. Trailers are not occupied when traveling, so there is no need to have the steps automatically extend or retract every time the door opens or closes. Fifth-wheel trailers seem to have the most steps.

Stairs in and out of any rig may create mobility issues, but there are add-ons such as personal lifts available. Even a simple step stool can help.

- **Recommendation**: Be aware of door width and obstacles. Otherwise, it is your choice.

- **Rationale**: We prefer the front entrance because it gives a longer continuous wall behind the door. Some prefer the mid-ship because it gives an entry point closer to the kitchen area instead of walking around the front chairs. Two considerations on the front entrance are the door width and the path past a front mounted TV. If you bump your head on the TV or have to duck to get around it, then, you will want a mid-ship door or realign, relocate, or remove the TV.

Slides and room extensions may occur on either side of the rig, and we will discuss the slides when we get to the driver's side.

Basement Storage Bays are either side-to-side pass-through or box-style bins or a combination of both. The diesel pushers will have more opportunity for side-to-side pass-through because there is no driveline to block the storage. Think of the baggage storage on a Greyhound or other commercial buses. If the storage bins are attached to any slides and move out with the slide, these will be the box style. With these slides, you may have to be concerned with the weight of the articles stored in the bins.

We have talked to people who have burned up the slide motors more than once because of combined weight in the cargo area and interior slideout storage. If you are fortunate enough to find pass-through basement storage you might want to consider commercial steel drawers for those storage areas. The drawers will let you load or unload from either side and save the effort of crawling under a slide to retrieve that needed item. Finally, notice if the doors to your storage are hinged at the top or front of the bin.

Doors that open hinged at the top have the danger of being destroyed if they are left open beneath a slide when closing the slide. Yes, it happens! The doors hinged at the front have no such problem and are hinged at the front to prevent opening in transit.

- **Recommendation**: Either is adequate for storage and neither ought to be a "deal-killer." Pass-through is the best and box bins are okay. Know what you want to put into your storage and go with your storage needs.

- **Rationale**: We have had both the box style bin that travels with the slide and the pass-through storage. We like the pass-through for weight distribution and ease of accessing all areas of any pass-through. Also, there is no weight consideration for the slide operation.

Awnings for Patio come in two standard designs. First is the manually opened and closed awning. The manual style uses what is called an awning pull rod or awning hook. By releasing a lock mechanism on the forward end of the roller and pulling on a woven ribbon, you can open the awning. Then lock it down, extend the supports on either end, and adjust the supports to either lock onto the side of the rig, or detach and be secured to the ground. This process is easier to do than to describe. Your dealer or seller will show you how to do it. If you have the manual style awning, we emphatically recommend you have safety clamps that lock around the rolled up awning to prevent the wind from unfurling it on the highway at 60-MPH. These safety straps are listed as an RV Awning Clamp® by Camco and can be installed by the dealer or you. Along with the patio awning are window awnings.

- **Recommendation**: We recommend installing awnings on the bedroom, dining, and livingroom windows.

- **Rationale**: Awnings provide sun and rain protection, and privacy. They are deployed with an awning hook.

The rear end of the rig will be configured based on engine placement or, in the case of trailers, for the possibility of additional towing.

Motorized

If the rig has a diesel engine, you will see the radiator plus oil and transmission fluid dip sticks and perhaps a sight-glass to see the coolant level. If the engine's radiator is a side mounted radiator you will see the belts, engine, the transmission and oil dipsticks and the sight-glass for coolant level. You may also see the hydraulic reservoirs and somewhere close by will be the oil filters.

If the rig is a gas engine in the front, you will probably have access to the onboard generator at the rear. Usually motorized vehicles will have a receiver for towing.

Towable

If you are looking at the back end of a trailer or fifth-wheel, you may or may not have a hitch receiver. Some states allow for towing doubles, check the states you will be traveling in or through as well as your home state laws. The rear of a trailer may have a large picture window – nice!

Since the rear end of a towed vehicle has nothing to do with te mechanics of the trailer, it is strictly up to you. Fifth-wheels tend to have larger windows and many times the whole back end is a window.

- **Recommendation**: If you are looking at a diesel pusher the side mounted radiator is your best option, and a rear radiator is acceptable as long as you know that changing a belt may cost upwards of $1,200. All towable end caps are acceptable either with or without the picture window. Fifth-wheels will have the largest window in the rear. Which trailer is your choice based on what best meets your needs and budget.

- **Rationale**: The side radiator gives service personnel more access to your engine without going through the inside of you coach. Belts and parts of the engine are accessible through the grill. If the radiator takes up the rear access, nothing about the engine is available through the grill area except the fluid dipsticks. You don't want technicians with greasy or oily clothes or shoes going back and forth through your bedroom. Mechanics have told us that no matter how much they protect your stuff there is bound to be oil or grease transfer, as well as a more costly bill.

Slides and room extensions may be on either side or both sides of the RV, so if you have slides on the passenger side go back to that side and apply this information where appropriate.

There are several mechanisms that manufacturers use to extend and retract the slides. You will also need to check the interior of the slide to estimate the weight load the slide carries. If it is a kitchen slide with a residential refrigerator and pantry storage, consider the weight of canned goods as opposed to dry goods.

Slide mechanisms include hydraulic, electric cable, electric screw style extender, or electric gear motors that follow a track. Virtually all mechanisms can be overridden in case of failure. Although the manual over-ride is there, you never want to have to use it! Depending on the weight and size of the slide they will have different support mechanisms. The slide will probably ride on two or more rails, and these need lubricating with a lubricant recommended by the manufacturer.

Slides also have rubber gaskets on the sides, top, and bottom. These rubber gaskets are the primary defense against encroaching moisture, whether the slide is open or closed. Treat them well, and they will help you stay dry. Finally, the slides may have "Toppers." Toppers are an awning like covering that extends and retracts with the slide. Their primary purpose is to keep water from pooling on the flat top of the slide as well as keeping junk, such as leaves and debris from falling onto the slide and compromising the top rubber gasket.

You may decide to get a Class A with a full-side slide. This large slide is relatively new in the industry. Our caution on the full-side slide is that, once your RV is loaded it may put more weight on the front axle, potentially exceeding the recommended GVWR (see Chapter 5). What this means is that you might have to lighten the frontend load. Full-side slides are great when open, but may cause problems in some RV parks or resorts, even in our favorite campground, Walmart parking lot. Because of some of the issues we have heard from owners of full-side slides, we can only wonder if the slide will hold up in the long run. One owner we talked to has a full-side slide with no opposing slide. He commented the slide tended to un-level the coach when he extended it because there was no counterweight on the opposite side. Motorhomes and trailers torque when going down the road, up and down driveways, and entrances to parking lots. It seems to us that the longer the slide, the more chance of torquing and needing realignment or repair. When in use full-side slides are awesome.

We have seen fifth-wheel trailers that have as many as five slides. The caution here is that one switch may run all five slides in sequence. You cannot control the slides one at a time. It is all or nothing!

How much more room will the slide give you? If you have the kitchen in a slide, the chances are it is a very shallow slide. That is, it may only go out twelve to fifteen inches. If you opt for the kitchen slide, remember that all the electric, gas, water, and waste lines have to be designed to go in and out countless times. The more stuff that is going in and out the better the chance of one or more systems failing. On the other hand, if the livingroom and dining areas extend, then you will have electricity moving in and out, and the slide will have the ability to go out as much as three feet. Greater space with less chance of system failures.

- **Recommendation**: Get an RV with slides. They are ideal for expanding the living space and reducing "pinch-points" when moving around. We recommend at least two slides, even if you get the full-side slide. We also recommend that you get the one that extends the most.

  We prefer the hydraulic extenders over the gear driven or worm drive. We recommend the kitchen is not the only slide. Many of the larger fifth-wheel trailers will have the kitchen within the extendable area, so, in this instance, watch your slide weight. Get slides that you can control one at a time.

- **Rationale:** We have had rigs with and without slides. The extra room is an affordable amenity. We have talked to people who have burned up more than one motor either extending or retracting their slide due to the weight of stored items. But, we haven't heard from anyone who has had trouble with hydraulic driven slides. As far as the depth of the slide or the length, our recommendation and rationale are given in our above discussion. It is for you to determine what you want. We have seen slides that incorporated the kitchen fail more often than any other slide area. True of fifth-wheels and motorhomes. This failure may be due to excessive weight, the slide motor, or the number of components moving in and out.

Utility Bays contain the sewer connections for black and grey water rinse and discharge as well as fresh water hookup. Look for a clean compartment without any signs of leakage. Also, check to make sure you have enough room for the sewer hose storage. If there isn't space for the drain hose, find out where you can store it safely and conveniently. There are aftermarket tubes for storage that will work if you can discover a good spot to mount them.

Electrical, phone, and cable connections will be located in an adjoining bay.

- **Recommendation**: Avoid sewer drain systems that have a built-in macerator.
- **Rationale:** Macerators empty the tanks slowly rather than getting a good flushing rush of water. A full tank drains best because the water flows with force.

Front End Cap inspection is one of those things to put on your regular maintenance program. How frequently you inspect depends on where you go and how often. Rough roads, windy conditions and who you are following will make a difference. If you follow trucks that have recently joined the paved road, you may suffer from glass chips or breakage.

When you are looking at a rig on the lot or private seller's driveway, notice any small glass chips. These will vary in size from a small fraction of an inch (1/32) which cannot be repaired, to larger stone chips that have started to spread by way of spider cracks. These can be fixed if "less than a dollar bill" in size. All chips ought to be professionally epoxied before you take possession. The windshield is an integral part of the roof structure. As long as the glass is in its frame, you should be okay but check with an RV glass company to make sure. Two piece windshields are about one half the cost of replacing a single full windshield.

After you have looked at the windshield, look for stress cracks in the fiberglass front cap. If the front is metal, you are probably okay. Check for water leakage around the window gasket and the clearance lights. Have everything sealed with the appropriate sealing material, usually silicone. One of the best repair materials we have found for stress cracks is the plastic glue that is activated by ultra-violet light. If using it outside, work at night or very quickly, the Sun produces ultra-violet light. Some manufacturers protect the lower portion of the front cap against stone chips with additional clear materials.

- **Recommendation**: Have windshields repaired or replaced before you take position. Inspect and care for small damage before it becomes larger.Fill fiberglass stress cracks wherever they are with the five-second glue.

- **Rationale**: Stress cracks are expensive to have repaired, and repair businesses advise that the cracks will return in a short time. Better to relieve the stress as long as it is sealed against water intrusion.

Generators in motorhomes are pretty much standard, and the common is Onan, a Cummins company. Check the exhaust area. If you are looking at a built-in generator in a motorized or trailer unit, notice where the exhaust pipe is located. Does it allow fumes to drift into your living or sleeping space? If so, you will want to vent it up and away.

Gas driven vehicles have the motor's exhaust pipe mid-ship and the generator at the rear of the RV. On diesel driven vehicles the engine exhaust will be at the rear and the generator at the very front. There are after-market products that will safely transport the fumes from your generator up, up, and away. One such product is called Gen-turi® Generator Exhaust System. This or similar products will be appreciated by neighbors, especially if you are at an RV rally or get together.

If your generator is portable, you will want to place it close enough and lock it to your RV to protect it from theft. We have talked to too many people who have had their portable generators stolen even when chained or cabled to their trailer. Perhaps the best location is locked in the bed of the tow vehicle, or even inside the tow vehicle when not using it. Getting the right size portable generator is as important as having the right size installed in your rig. A portable generator such as Honda® with an output of 3000+ watts will probably suffice in most circumstances. If your air conditioner is rated at 15-18 amps, with a starting amperage of 20-22 amps, and you have a 2000 watt (or 2KW) generator, then you stand a chance of burning the A/C motor because, at start-up, it will draw more power than the generator can handle. This condition results in a brown-out during the starting of the A/C. Too much power is better than too little. Here is a formula you can use: Amp = Watt ÷ Volt.

- **Recommendation**: Find out what the starting amperage is for the A/C or other motors that are operating when the A/C starts. Then divide the total amperage by 120V and see if the output exceeds the startup demand.

- **Rationale**: It's all about math. If you want, have an expert help calculate the startup amperage and find out what size generator you need. Don't kid yourself into buying or getting a generator that is too underpowered. It is better to have too much than not enough.

Top of the rig is where you may want help. You will need to climb the ladder that is attached to the RV. If there is no ladder then use a separate ladder. Caution, if there is no ladder attached to the

RV, the manufacturer probably doesn't want you walking around on the roof. In that case, do your inspection from the ladder. Look for wear and tear, any gouges, patch repairs, or serious scrapes which may need further investigation. If you prefer, have a professional inspect the roof. This information applies to all RVs. Fifth-wheels, trailers, and motorhomes all have pretty much the same roof components.

If it is a rubber roof, is it chalky, dark colored, or cracked? If so have a person you trust evaluate the roof condition. Check for repairs and maintenance on the roof. Look at the seams and around any pipes or equipment such as A/C units that penetrate the roof. Has the roof and caulking been maintained? Our best information is that a rubber roof needs to be cleaned, have a protectant sprayed on it and all joints inspected or caulked twice a year.

If you have a fiberglass roof, you will need to check the joints and caulk where necessary. We still like to clean and protect the roof twice a year, whether it needs it or not. Branches can scratch the roof, knock caps off vents and damage other roof items.

If you are buying a travel trailer, then you have little to inspect, especially if the roof is metal. Once again, check for possible leaks and caulk as necessary. Also, consider having the dealer run a pressure test to find potential leaks in the roof where the walls meet it and where anything comes up through the roof. Basically and oversimplified, the dealer will pressurize the coach and spray soapy water on the roof then watch for bubbles.

Some coaches and many trailers have a metal roof, look for missing screws or rivets, cuts, dings, or dents. Here again, look for caulking and proper maintenance. If the rig is new, there won't be much to see, but look at it so you know how a roof ought to look. If the rig is used, look for all the items we have already covered and then look for scratches that may have worn through the paint or enamel. Use touch up paint as needed to prevent the elements from destroying the metal and causing interior damage.

All this inspection may seem as though we are too fussy, but water and RVs do not get along well. The water always wins. In the end, if you are buying from a dealer, talk to your salesperson and the service manager about roof maintenance. We will be looking at the ceiling later and double checking for water damage from the inside.

Bottom of the rig beginning with the tires. If you are inspecting a motorhome, regardless of classification, you will find either four, six, or eight tires. Each tire is stamped at the factory with the creation or "birthdate." Look for the DOT stamp and the four numbers following the DOT. Those four numbers represent the week and year of manufacture. The first two are the week the tire was made, and the last two are the year. If the tire were built before 2000, you would see a different coding, but don't concern yourself with "before 2000." Remember that most RV tires have about a four-year life expectancy regardless of tread wear.

What else is under there? On Class A and the larger Class C, and even on the Super B, you may have leveling jacks. Check the jacks when they are down for leaking seals and deteriorating rubber. While you are taking a peek underneath, look for drips and signs of leakage anywhere under the RV. No need to crawl under, just be observant. Watch the jacks come down and then retract. Notice if one or more is sluggish. We have noticed that some motorhomes have three jacks, two in the back and one in the front.

If you are inspecting a fifth-wheel or travel trailer, you might want to check the tire age on these rigs. Tires that sit are unhappy tires. Tires were meant to roll and flex and let the natural oils move around. Sidewalls that are sun checked are in need of replacement. Tire dealers have told us that you can extend the tire's life expectancy by covering them with a tire covers. Another way to lengthen the tire's life is to put the jacks down to take the load off the tires when in storage so they do not develop a flat spot from too much resting. Remember, a rolling tire is a happy tire.

One of the easiest things to look for under trailers is the plumbing. Look for pipes that will drain. Sewer lines ought to slope towards the sewer connection. Also, check to see if there is a supporting metal strap under the holding tanks. We have seen new trailers with a sagging support strap several inches below the holding tanks. Imagine what might happen with a full holding tank and a good bump in the road with the support catching the falling holding tank! Remember, a punch has more force than a push.

Many fifth-wheels have multiple sewer lines running to one or more hookup points. Understand how to hook these lines to the shore-side sewer system. If the kitchen is in the rear and the bathroom is in the front, you will have to empty the forward blackwater tank, rinse the drain hose with the forward gray water, then move ahead at a dump station and empty the kitchen gray water. If you are in a campground, you may have to have two hoses connected to a "Y" and a third hose to the sewer hookup.WOW!

Other than those few items, there isn't much to see. Other items are for a more sophisticated inspection by a qualified technician or mechanic. These more in-depth inspections might include air bags, wheel bearings, packing, and seals, brakes, and any wires or hoses hanging down from underneath the trailer.

Travel trailers are closer to the ground so may be harder to see what is going on underneath. Don't be too concerned because there is usually less to see or go wrong. The suggestions about having a mechanic or technician are just as valid with a travel trailer as with the fifth-wheel. This in-depth inspection is probably something you will want to leave to the pros.

With the Class A, B, and C motorized models, there is an engine, and it should be tested and serviced. Testing can be done with an engine oil analysis. It's advisable to establish a baseline of all services as soon as you obtain your new rig, especially if you have an extended warranty. With the smaller engines, the cost of a tune-up and fluid change is not going to be too much to spend on your new motorhome.

All the considerations regarding looking under a Class A rig apply to B's and C's, and it may be easier when it is up on a service lift. Don't forget to check the transmission and have it serviced. If you are going to pull or tow something, consider a transmission cooler as an added protection against overheating.

- **Recommendation**: Rremember to examine your going-to-be-new rig, and set a baseline for maintenance. Have an expert mechanic or technician examine what you cannot. And, finally, purchase an extended warranty even if you are buying a new rig. Check with the extended warranty company to determine the best time to buy.

- **Rationale**: Mechanical things break, and the bill for repairs motorhomes and to a lesser extent on trailers can hurt your wallet. A small ding that is nothing more than cosmetic has the potential to let moisture leak into the framework and may cost $1,500 or more to repair. Buyer Beware.

CHAPTER 9 / The Interior Walkthrough

The exterior determines what you will be living in; the interior determines how comfortable you will be in your mobile residency. Whether travel trailer, fifth-wheel or motorhome you will find things you would like but cannot seem to find. Your choice is to have your rig modified to suit your tastes or, as most do, make concessions and live with some things you might want to change. Your best bet is to make a list of the must-haves, negotiables, and deal-breakers. Combine this list with your exterior list.

Your list does not need to be massive, but merely what you want and what you don't want and what you can afford. By our third motorhome, we had our list of sixteen items, which we had to have, were negotiable, or were deal-breakers. We ended up with ten wants of the sixteen, six negotiables, and no deal breakers.

As we review what you might find, we will point out some things we found to be negative but may be positive to you. Our purpose is simply to raise your awareness. Choose what is important to you.You probably will never find any motorhome or trailer that has everything you want. Some negatives are simply the nature of the beast regardless of style or manufacturer.

When you walk into an RV, you may be entranced by the WOW factor. Wow, it looks so big. Wow, look at all the cabinets. Wow, it feels elegant, or homey, or comfortable, etc. Now, leave that impression at the door. Look at each of the components and ask if it will be what you want to make life livable on the road.

Notice the color or tone of the interior. Within the past few years, manufacturers have decided dark or black wood cabinets, and trim is the color of the day. We have been in some very nice rigs, motorhomes, fifth-wheels, and travel trailers that are darker with all the lights on than our Maple appointed motorhome is with all the lights off! Look at the floor. Is the flooring light or dark? Is the ceiling dark or light? The darkness of dark wood trim is okay for some, but ask yourself if it is right for you.

The ceiling may be a single piece of the architecture or divided into sections. Notice what type of ceiling is in the rig. Some are 4-foot sections supported by "T" bars like a drop ceiling in a building. Others are finished wood or simulated wood; some are carpeted. Regardless of ceiling type, look around the A/C or other openings. This area is where you will see evidence of water intrusion. If you see something that is suspicious, ask for information regarding potential damage.

If the ceiling is a sectioned ceiling, and the sections are held in place by "T" bars, look carefully to ensure that the sections are flat rather than sagging. A sagging section can slip out of the support and fall. Once the sections sag, they will need to be replaced. Yes, it does happen, we have seen some expensive rigs with this problem.

The livingroom may have rope lighting around a mirror which does not contribute to the overall brightness of the room. Consider the look of the ceiling. Most are closer to your head than in a regular home. The exception would be fifth-wheel trailers that have a sloping ceiling from front to back. A mirror on the ceiling in the livingroom of a MH may seem pretty neat until you have to clean it, especially if there is even a small amount of cooking grease on the mirror.

Flooring is next. If your RV has tiles on the floor, usually reserved for motorhomes having a chassis that can carry that extra weight, check the size of the tiles. Sixteen-inch tiles may crack and break when the rig twists. They are just too large to last the life of the RV. On the other hand, twelve-inch tiles seem to hold up very well.

If your rig has linoleum flooring, check to make sure the flooring is glued down all the way around and throughout the coach or trailer. Look for bubbles and notice soft spots.

- **Recommendation**: Your choice. What floor will fit with your lifestyle is the issue here. Perhaps a mix of flooring may be best.

- **Rationale**: We are divided here. We have tile in the kitchen and bath area and carpeting in the dining and livingroom. Unless you have an Aqua-Hot® system, the tile can be cold in the morning and may be slippery if wet, but it is easy to clean. On the other hand, the carpet is warm in the morning, and harder to keep clean. Our carpet has soaked up some large spills and cleaned without too much trouble.

The walls ought to be good construction and flat without bubbles or separation. If you press on any interior wall, you can usually feel it give on both sides because it is hollow. Now is a good time to reiterate the fact that motorhomes and trailers are built a certain way because manufacturers have found a building style and components that work. Just because a wall is hollow does not mean it won't work as intended. These are not bearing walls and may seem to be flimsy, but their purpose is to divide space.

Fixtures in all sinks, basins, and counters should be checked to see that all are sealed or caulked. This sealing or caulking is an ongoing project that you can do yourself with little difficulty. If the caulking has open spaces when you are looking and evaluating one of two things has occurred. If it is a used RV, the former owners may not have paid attention to maintenance in this area, and water damage could be present. If the unit is new, then the manufacturer didn't complete the job, and the dealer will need to do the caulking.

We have met people who purchased a fifth-wheel toy-hauler, and the owner wanted to do the minor fixes himself. The sales person pointed out that if the buyer started fixing things, it could have an impact on the warranty. If a new purchase, leave all repairs to the dealership.

Just like in a fixed foundation home, the kitchen is the workplace in the RV. The sink will be one of several materials, from porcelain, plastic or fiberglass, to stainless. Kitchen sinks will have all the configurations you would expect in any kitchen. It's your choice here, but remember some materials such as plastic or fiberglass stain or crack, others do not.

The faucets may be an inexpensive plastic or a higher grade regular home faucet from Moen, Delta, or other quality fixture.

The stove may be a two or three burner propane stove with an oven, or it may be a two or three burner cooktop with a microwave or convection oven above the cooking surface. Those with a cooktop will probably not have an oven. Some of the newer RVs have a glass top cooking surface, and a very few may have an induction cooking surface.

Again, it is what you feel comfortable using, but take notice, so you won't be disappointed later. If you are looking at several rigs or looking over a length of time, take pictures with your phone or camera and catalog the photos for later reference.

- **Recommendation**: Enamel or stainless steel sinks with good heavy duty fixtures. These may be a drop-in and slightly raised from the counter surface or mounted from underneath the counter surface. We prefer the residential style faucet and fixtures.

- **Rationale:** Plastic or fiberglass sinks stain easily and are hard to keep looking new through the years. Faucets need replacement parts, and the RV faucets tend to be a "throwaway" item when they get worn. Residential faucets can be repaired at a fraction of the cost of replacement.

Water and waste capacities can be a critical consideration if you are planning to boondock for more than a day or two. For the past several years we have consistently used about nine gallons of water per day per person. This water consumption includes a shower each day for the two of us and our pets. It also includes water for drinking, cooking, and cleaning dishes. And finally it includes flushing the toilet. Make sure you consider the water capacities of the RV you are looking at and whether your time will be spent in campgrounds with hookups or on the road operating in the self-contained mode.

- **Recommendation**: Water storage cannot easily be expanded later on, so we recommend you have enough water on board for the kind of camping you will usually be doing. With conservation of water you may be able to boondock a week or more.

- **Rationale:** Your intended camping style will dictate how much water storage you need. Use 10-gal./person/day multiplied by the number of days you will go between refilling your fresh water and flushing your waste tanks.

Kitchen lighting ought to be bright and adequate for cooking and clean-up.

- **Recommendation**: White LED bullet type lighting or LED fluorescents.

- **Rationale**: LEDs are much cooler, and more power conservative. The LED gives off plenty light to illuminate you're food preparation, cooking, and cleaning areas. LEDs tend to be pricey, so may have to be replaced a few at a time.

Kitchen cabinets are the next things you need to consider. Manufacturers may load you down with drawers. Drawers here, there, and everywhere. Look at the number of drawers in the kitchen as well as observing their depth. Consider what you will put into the drawers. If the drawers are too shallow, they won't hold pots and pans. If too deep the bottom may sag and eventually fall out of the drawer sides or they may slide open during travel. Remember, your RV is like a stick and brick home in a hurricane during an eight to ten magnitude earthquake! Things shift. Shelving and drawer bottoms are subject to more stress in a moving environment than a home on a foundation. So, be sure shelves and drawers are adequately supported and that everything will stay put most of the time when you are going down the road.

Scrutinize the storage for pots, pans, food, and utensils. Know what you want to take and decide where it will all go.

- **Recommendation**: Solid wood overhead cabinets well anchored to the ceiling and wall or the countertop and wall. The cabinet sides may be thin 1/8 plywood, but the corners ought to be substantial and more than just glued and stapled.

- **Rationale:** Cabinets and drawers need to be well constructed and anchored to hold much more weight than will be put into them. We have had overhead cabinets break free of the anchoring system due to twisting of the MH going over inclines such as parking access and driveways at something other than a 90-degree angle. A bouncing weight is heavier than its still weight counterpart. Think about the force of a pounding hammer vs a pushing hammer.

Refrigerators in RVs have evolved from the RV fridges made by Norcold® and Dometic® to residential ones you might find in any appliance store. Our Dometic side by side holds enough food, fresh and frozen, for about one month for the two of us. About the only thing, we need to stock up on short-term are eggs and milk. If you have a residential refer, then you will be able to hold a lot more, and you'll have to learn how to pack it so food items don't slide around, tip over, or fall out when you open the door. It can be done, it's just another thing to check when you are ready to move out. Residential refrigerators are usually big enough to hold food for a family of five or six.

- **Recommendation**: We prefer the tried and true RV refrigerators made for gas or electric use and made for traveling.

- **Rationale**: The residential refrigerators we have seen in use used only a small portion of their intended capacity.

  We are mostly concerned about the replacement problems with these larger appliances. Household refrigerators necessitate using shore power, a generator, or solar power with a large inverter and battery system. A downside to the residential refrigerator is removal and replacement from the rig if replacement is necessary. There are two options we know of, through the windshield or removing the slide. Either method of removal can be thousands of dollars in addition to the cost of a new appliance.

According to research on repairing or replacing residential fridges be prepared for this eventuality within a three to seven year window. The newer models are built to run continuously which may become a problem when on the road.

Bathrooms can be the best or the worst of situations. Usually, the toilet room, commode, or water closet, if you prefer, is narrow. Many toilets are lower than the household toilet you may be used to. Sit on the toilet and close the door. If you are comfortable, then it is okay, but if it is too narrow keep looking. If the toilet seat is too close to the floor, consider replacing with one that has a higher seat. The water closet may have a basin, the same observations applies here as with the kitchen sink.

The shower and a second basin will probably be located in the same area or the toilet may not be separated from the bathroom as a whole.

Take your shoes off and stand in the shower. We like to measure showers and shower surrounds by putting our hands on our hips akimbo and turning around. If we don't touch any of the surround, then the shower will be big enough to use without compromise. While you are in the shower or tub, notice any soft spots in the shower or tub floor. These soft spots may become problem areas in the future.

One or two? If the bathroom is in the back of the motorhome, you will have a second "powder room" or half-bath forward so you can use the toilet without opening the bedroom slide.

Fifth-wheels usually have the bath at the top of the interior stairs to the bedroom, and can usually be accessed from the stairs or the bedroom. Travel trailers may have the bath in the rear and a second door leading directly outside. This door is a nice touch if you need to come in from swimming or are wet from rain or are dirty. This arrangement keeps the living space cleaner.

- **Recommendation**: Having 1-1/2 baths cuts the waiting-to-use time. Be sure the shower is big enough, and the sinks conform to your desires. This advice applies to all forms of RVs.

- **Rationale**: One bathroom can cause a jam at the water closet and can create a "pinch-point" for through traffic to or from the bedroom. A bath in the rear of the MH creates a step up from the bedroom to the bath. This may be preferable to a ledge on the back side of the bed. Trailers may have their own "pinch-points" so be aware of where they may be, whether kitchen, hall, or bath.

The Bedroom only refers to the area sectioned off from the rest of the RV and not to all the potential sleeping locations such as a drop-down table or sofa. We call beds that have their axis parallel to the RV as North-South and beds with an axis perpendicular to the rig's axis as East-West. Fifth-wheel trailers will almost always be the East-West configuration and may have a slide in the bedroom that is either the bed or a wardrobe. This slide gives enough room to walk around the bed rather than crawling over it to get to whatever is on the other side. Travel trailers may be in either configuration, but the area may be virtually occupied from wall to wall by the bed.

Bedrooms will have the nightstands built in and very close to the bed's mattress. If the nightstand is deep from front to back, it creates a problem making the bed. The best option is to have the bed-maker imagine making the bed, stretching around the nightstand and tucking sheets and linens between the nightstand and the tight fitting mattress. We have found the shorter nightstands make housekeeping easier.

If the bed is in an East-West configuration in a diesel pusher, there may be a ledge on the back side that is so tall it puts the mattress at floor level on that side of the bed. This ledge is usually about a foot wide, so the bed-maker must kneel down to make that side of the bed. Getting in and out of bed with a high ledge can be a daily challenge. A caveat here is, if the MH has a rear bath the floor around the bed will be level and the rise to accommodate the engine will be below the bathroom floor. Therefore, you will have a step up to the bathroom.

If the bed is in the North-South configuration there will be a narrow walking space on both sides of the bed, but, again, the nightstands may make bed making problematic. Many bedrooms with North-South beds may not have a slide since there is little need to expand the room to allow access from both sides of the bed.

- **Recommendation**: We like the North-South configuration as long as the aisles on either side of the bed allow for walking, turning around and making the bed. The bed will usually be a full-size or queen rather than a king size bed. East-West configurations are fine as long as the ledge isn't more than six inches or so in height.

- **Rationale**: It comes down to cramped quarters and having to perform housekeeping in the bedroom. Check out the space **and** built-ins in the bedroom to ensure you are satisfied with being able to do more than sleep. Nightstands are usually too tight to make bed-making easy. Remember that the designers of the interior space have probably never spent a night in their creations.

CHAPTER 10 / Driving Tips

We do not pretend to be driving instructors nor do we have the best information on how to drive your rig. Three things to be aware of are, tail-swing, off-tracking, and adjusting your mirrors for proper rearview placement. Remember many places are large-rig unfriendly. Parking lots sometimes offer little turning room from lane to lane. Even with a travel trailer or fifth-wheel, you are NOT driving your family auto.

Regardless of the years, you have behind the wheel driving your daily car, driving anything bigger than a pickup truck, or van is different than what you might be used to handling. As mentioned earlier van conversions and Class B's will take minimal adjustment. They can virtually go anywhere your SUV can go, and can be parked anywhere you can park your car. Class C's and A's and some towables will be more challenging.

When we bought our first MH, a 1991 31-foot Class A rig, it seemed as big as the Queen Mary. We had to learn to watch for obstacles on both sides as well as our vertical clearance. Road signs sometimes lean out into the road past the curb, tree branches hang down and grow close to the ground. You might have noticed that trees lining streets seem to be pruned to a particular height. Chances are they were pruned by buses and trucks, not a road crew. Our first rig was 11'4" high, and even at that low height, we needed to be aware of potential obstacles. One of our first adventures was an attempt to take it under a bridge that had a 10'8" clearance. It didn't work! The remains of our front A/C needed to be professionally removed, and a new one installed. Our next adventure was backing into a tree. Apparently, the tree jumped out in the way of the rear overhang of the MH. A bent bumper was easily fixed. Here is a rule you can take away from this sort of accident. **G.O.A.L.** stands for **G**et **Out And L**ook. If you don't have a co-pilot to guide you, you will have to assess space and clearances for yourself. Measure the rig's highest point and add a few inches for good measure. Put a label on your dash to let anyone who drives the RV know how high it is. Sometimes the road will be resurfaced diminishing the actual clearance, but the clearance signs aren't changed.

We firmly recommend attending one of the RV driving schools taught by qualified instructors. Some dealers offer a short driving course when you purchase a rig from them. This dealer offered course may be for free or fee, either way, take advantage of the opportunity to learn. Some organizations offer RV driving classes that are well worth the money. In the meantime, here are some suggestions.

There are several videos on YouTube describing tail swing and off tracking as well as mirror placement. Two that we recommend can be seen here.

https://www.youtube.com/watch?v=mdrx8oSH2pc

Or here:

https://www.youtube.com/watch?v=y5MSGqfh8z0

Setting your mirrors to give you maximum information is another important consideration before you drive off. Flat mirrors are like any flat mirror, they tell you what is approaching you from behind. The convex mirrors show you what is behind and around you. Adjusting these mirrors is an operation for two people even if your mirrors are power mirrors. You will need help determining where your rear wheels are in the convex mirrors. An outside helper can do this for you. You will have a fairly large blind spot on the curb or passenger side. This blind spot is large enough to hide a car, and you will want to know where it begins and ends. Ask your dealer for help in mirror adjustment when you get your new rig. It only takes a few minutes and is well worth the time when you consider the safety issues. You can find information on mirror adjustment at:

http://hubpages.com/sports/Adjusting-your-RV-MIRRORs

Backing your rig into spaces, whether campground or other areas can be challenging. In our case, any time we need to back almost any time the co-pilot is outside on the ground and is actually in control of the backing procedure. The pilot's job is to follow the directions and trust the co-pilot to guide properly and avoid things on the ground, overhead, and sides that could cause problems. If the pilot sees something that the co-pilot might have missed, we stop and review what is going on and confirm everything is okay.

It seems, when you are parking in a back-in space in a campground, you are the entertainment, and once backed in others after you become your entertainment!

By having clear and visible hand signals, you can lose your audience in short order. Here is how we do it. The co-pilot always keeps the mirrors in view. If you can't see the mirror, the pilot cannot see you. That means moving with the rig, don't just stand in one spot. Arm signals work best for us. Small finger or slight hand signals are hard to see from 40-50 feet away, especially in dim light. Two arms work better than one and crossed arms always means stop. Oh yes, construction workers and crane operators use finger and fist signals, but unless that is you, use easy to interpret gestures. We took our signals from the airline industry, and those signals have worked well for us. Here is another hint. If folks try and help you and you know and trust your co-pilot, just let them know you would be happy to let them help right after they sign an agreement where they assume all responsibility and liability for any damage to your rig or anything it hits.

We don't have such an agreement, and no one has ever said, "Sure, I'll be responsible for any damage. Where do I sign?"

CHAPTER 11 / Before you leave

Now that you are armed and ready to purchase your new rig there are a few very important items you will need for a safe and repair-free time. No, it won't really be repair free, but these small items will help you have an easier time along the road.

A Surge protector is a must-have every time you plug into shore-power. Electric pedestals are notorious for having questionable power at every site regardless of how highly the campground is rated.

- **Recommendation**: We have talked to too many travelers who have had encounters with the pedestal. What could go wrong? Almost anything having to do with electricity.

- **Rationale:** Some of the issues we have seen are power surges, power brownouts, and incorrect polarity with neutral and ground wires reversed. The difference between a surge protector and nothing can be blowing your circuit control panels, motherboards and burning motors without protection, or no problems with one. Expect to pay $400 or so for a good one. They can be mounted in your coach or plugged in-line on your power cord.

Water filters are connected in line between shore water or city water and your rig. These are the inexpensive blue filters by Camco which can be purchased at Walmart or any RV supply store.

- **Recommendation**: Always connect to city water through one of these filters whether you are filling your fresh water or using shore water.

- **Rationale:** Every water source has small bits of sand or undissolved solids in it. These small solids are not harmful to use or consume, but they can disrupt your water system. There are two back-check valves in an RV system. One is between the fresh water and the pump, and the other is at the city water connection. If either of these has a grain of sand that is trapped in the valve your system will cycle the pump on and off, on and off until the sand is cleared. One caution is the first time you use the filter turn the water on and let it run a few seconds to clear the carbon in the filter before connecting to your RV.

Water hydrants can become cross contaminated too easily and without your knowledge. We have seen campers wash out the grey and black water through their sewer hose and then place the sewer hose over the faucet to rinse. Yuck! They just left a contaminated faucet for you to use to fill your fresh water. What's more they turned the faucet on and off with a gloved hand they used to disconnect the sewer line. Double YUCK!

- **Recommendation:** We carry a container of Clorox® wipes and wipe down the faucet and the handle with the disinfectant before we touch any surface with our fill hose. By the way, you ought to have a white hose dedicated to fresh water and a different color for flushing the black tank or cleaning any surface around the dump area. If you can get fresh water away from the dump area use that source, but clean it with wipes.

- **Rationale:** Not everyone thinks about cross contamination. When the water source is close to the sewer dump area assume that the hydrant handle and faucet area are contaminated. Red handled hydrants are non-potable because they are located too close to the sewer or because the water is contaminated. Blue handled hydrants are safe for drinking water, but err on the side of health.

Water pressure regulators regulate the pressure of incoming water to your rig. City or well pressure may be higher than the recommended PSI for your RV. Many RV water pipes are rated by the manufacturers to withstand 40-50 PSI. Higher than normal pressure can affect pipe joints and cause leaks.

There are two types of regulators generally available. The first is a fixed setting around 40-50 PSI. The second is a variable setting that allows the user to dial the amount of pressure delivered to the RV.

- **Recommendation:** Put the regulator on first so it protects the hose, filter, and your system. Always use a pressure regulator if you will be using city water as the water source in your rig's plumbing. If you are just getting water for your fresh water tank it is unnecessary because you are not putting and pressure stress on the vented tank.

- **Rationale:** Always use a regulator as cheap insurance against water pressure damage. We feel the fixed setting is more reliable for two reasons. First, it is set at the factory and calibrated for RV water system pressure requirements. Second, the variable regulators have a tendency to break when it is most needed.

Awning de-flappers are an easy way dampen down the flapping canvas of an awning in windy conditions. This item is available at practically all RV stores. De-flappers are not useable on electric awnings because the mounting system is different.

- **Recommendation:** This is an easy item to install on manually operated awnings and will be beneficial in low to moderate wind.

- **Rationale:** De-flappers will save awnings from excessive billowing, vibration, and stress during windy conditions. They will also reduce the noise of the wind's effect on the awning.

Awning safety straps are one of the best safety devices you can install on your RV. They are a cable-like strap that completely secures your rolled up awning to the RV. The locks and straps that come with an awning are not necessarily sufficient to secure the awning from unfurling on the road at 60-MPH. Think liability.

- **Recommendation:** This is an inexpensive add-on that will save hundreds of dollars in repairs or replacement of your awning and rig.

- **Rationale:** There is the issue of damaging your own equipment and the potential for causing accidents because of a loose unfurled sheet of canvas hanging from the side of your RV.

Wheel covers are not a necessity, but they do contribute to extending the life of your tires and therefore making for a safer ride by decreasing sun damage to the tire's sidewalls.

- **Recommendation:** This is an easy way to extend the life expectancy of the tires.

- **Rationale:** Tire dealers recommend protecting tires from oxygen and sun damage with covers. This is a good way to save money by lengthening the tire's usefulness and safety.

A Transmission cooler is an additional cooling system to prevent the transmission from overheating.

- **Recommendation:** If you are towing a trailer or vehicle have your transmission equipped with a tow package.

- **Rationale: Transmissions** are installed by the manufacturer and designed to shift gears for that vehicle. Adding a towed trailer, fifth-wheel or other vehicle puts additional stress on the transmission and creates additional heat in the fluids. This excess heat can cause transmission failure.

CHAPTER 12 / Associations

Escapees is a membership site that is primarily informational but with plenty of social content. It has a lot of useful information and helps regarding discount parks, vehicle weight, and even assisted-living parks that are available to members.

We recommend this organization for its breadth and quality of information and resources available to members.

To sign up call 888-757-2582 or go online. Use our SKP number 106668 when you register, so SKP knows of our referral.

http://www.escapees.com/

FMCA stands for Family Motor Coach Association, and is a member site for folks who have a Class A, B, C, or bus conversion.

Again, we recommend this organization because of its breadth and quality of information relating to all types of motorhomes. There are how-to videos and commercial resources available to members. FMCA also has high-quality rallies throughout the country and year.

When joining let them know Jim and Loni Macy sent you! Our member number is F416786.

http://www.fmca.com/

RV Education 101 is one of the best websites you will find for RV maintenance. There are free videos and advice at the free membership level and additional videos for paid memberships.

We feel this is an essential resource for RVers. Remember, your RV is like having a home in an eight magnitude earthquake and a hurricane at the same time. Things get dislodged, don't work, or need replacement. This site gives practical information on how to complete any number of necessary repairs, from maintaining your sewer system, replacing hot water heaters, and who knows what else. The information is not intended to replace trained and qualified mechanics or technicians. It is there to help you evaluate whether you need a trained person or you can DIY.

http://www.rveducation101.com/

RV Village is a free membership site whose primary purpose is to provide a venue where RVers can get together socially on the Internet, in person, or on the road. This site is an excellent way to keep in touch with friends on the road to let them know where you are and how long you will be there.

We would recommend this site for its social value as well as a small commercial side where members can offer things for sale.

http://www.rvillage.com/home

CampingWorld is a company found throughout much of the United States specializing in RV sales and products. Although these are corporate stores, their pricing varies from location to location. It is our impression that CampingWorld's customer focus is toward the new RVer or the vacationer who uses their RV infrequently. Many products are available at other retailers at reduced prices. That said, it is a good investment to buy the CampingWorld® Good Sam® Membership. There are many benefits to membership, including in-store and online discounts, reduced fuel and propane prices, campground discounts, trip planning, roadside service, and medical emergency services, and insurance coverage geared specifically for the RVer.

http://goodsamclub.com/

http://campingworld.com/

RV Happy Hour is a social site which allows members to locate other nearby members. No charge to join. There are forums, groups, activities, and events. The map is questionable, but it is always undergoing improvement.

http://rvhappyhour.com.

IRV2 is a forum site. You can get in touch with others to help with many problems, from the engine to travel and information about campgrounds. This website has lots of good information from knowledgeable people. Membership has two levels, free and upgraded. This is good resource if you enjoy the forum genre. The site includes a classified section with both for sale and wanted items.

We recommend it for the informational content.

http://irv2.com/

Mobile RVing is a comprehensive park-finding website with extra bells and whistles. Here you will find trip planning, podcasts, blogs, and park reviews.

There is also the ability to look online at RV inventory and read descriptions so you have a better idea of what you want before you go to a dealer. Yup, we are very pro-dealer since we have had experience with both dealers and private-party sellers. Not that you can't get a good deal from a private party, especially if you invest in a thorough inspection from a reputable certified inspector.

https://www.mobilerving.com/

RoverPass is bare-bones site that will do a campground search for you and show any available discounts. This is a relatively new site and is updated on a regular basis. Not a bad deal for a minimum annual investment. Sure we belong, it's been worth it for us.

https://www.roverpass.com/roverpass-rv-club

Camping discounts are available through several membership programs and associations mentioned above. At the time of this writing, Passport America and Happy Camper both offer a 50% discount at participating campgrounds. You may also get a discount through AAA and other travel programs.

Free Camping in developed campgrounds or RV resorts is only available through membership campgrounds and affiliates. That means you buy a membership in a home-park campground and pay an annual maintenance fee to that park as long as you are a member.

Each membership park has its own contract and annual maintenance fee schedule. We recommend that you read the contract **before** you commit. The sales person may tell you what you want to hear, the **written word is what you get**. Those can be entirely different worlds!

Once you are a member, the park will offer you the ability to purchase programs allowing you to stay at affiliate campgrounds. These affiliate programs include Coast to Coast (C2C), Resort Parks International (RPI), Resorts of Distinction (ROD), Adventure Outdoor Resorts (AOR), and Thousand Trails (TT).

If you are just starting you might stick with Passport America, Happy Camper, or RoverPass until you decide whether the additional investment in a member park will save you camping money or cost you in membership expenses.

These issues are beyond the intended scope of this book, which is to help you buy an RV.

CHAPTER 13 / Recommended Companies

The following are companies we have used and have found to be reliable, fair in pricing, and have a high quality of work. They are not listed in any order that would indicate a priority of recommendation unless noted in the comments about the company. Our experience covers the Western U.S., so you will not find anything outside of our travel area at the time of writing.

RV Sellers

CampingWorld venues across the country. Mesa, AZ and Bakersfield, CA are two that we used in our search for a MH. Both give good useable information. A caveat here, not all CampingWorlds are alike. Prices differ as do manager's discounts.

http://campingworld.com

Guaranty RV in Junction City, OR is probably the most open and transparent company of any we have visited in the twelve western states. This company's inventory, financing resources, and integrity was what we needed when we bought our MH. Guaranty gets our highest recommendation. You may find the trip to OR to visit this company well worth it. The sales people offer complete and accurate information regarding questions you have, finding an RV that fits your lifestyle, and even helping you finance your purchase from them. This company has a stellar record with banks and credit unions and was recently named one of the top five dealers in the country. Finally, they have the mechanics, technicians, over 46 service, and paint shop bays to deal with any repair, seven days a week.

Guaranty also has a top-flight retail outlet complete with laundry facilities, and professional dog grooming, or a DIY area to groom your fur baby. You will find the staff friendly, courteous, personable and knowledgeable.

http://guarantyRV.com

RV Peddler in Bakersfield has a good selection of trailers and a few motorhomes. This business is family owned and local. They are knowledgeable and willing to work with their buyers. We have talked to the owner on several occasions, and she is upfront and willing to help.

http://rvpeddler.net

RV Repair

Allied Trailer Repair in Sacramento, CA is first on our list if you need work on your trailer or MH in the Sacramento area. We recommend them as a high-quality work facility. This company has been in the same location since the 1950's. Their work is excellent, and they are quick to respond to emergency repairs as well as the longer term renovations. Their pricing is well below some national companies. The building is vintage, but do not be dissuaded by looks.

http://www.alliedtrailerparts.com/

Cameron's Reliable Maintenance Service in Tucson, AZ is well-qualified to diagnose and make repairs from furnaces and refrigerators to Aqua-Hot® water systems and more. Ken Cameron has been servicing RVs for more than 15-years he is efficient and knowledgeable. He will respond to your location with a complete workshop to address your needs.

CampingWorld Collision repair in Bakersfield, CA, across the street from the retail store. They provide excellent work, fast, efficient, and take ownership of the needed repairs. Highly recommend for collision repair.

http://campingworld.com

Guaranty RV service in Junction City, OR has over 46-bays dedicated to chassis, interior, collision repair, and painting. Guaranty has mechanics trained in engine repair as well as technicians to complete the work you need to have done.

http://guarantyrv.com

Jerry & Keith's Truck Repair is our recommended place in Bakersfield, CA for diesel engine work from an oil change to major work. We have had our oil changed there on two occasions. Both times they were fast and checked out all grease fittings, oil filters, and filled with the oil we specified. Very fair in their pricing as well.

http://www.jerryandkeiths.com/

Mobile Maintenance & Towing in Tucson, AZ specializes in RV repair & towing. All RV's, diesel or gas. Repairs may be on site or in their shop. Qualified mobile mechanics are on duty day or night.

http://mmandt.net

TM Power Solutions in Tucson, AZ specializes in generator sales and service of RV generators including

Cummins, Generac, Kohler, and Onan. Provides onsite service and installations.

RV tires and alignment

Chicks Tire Service in Fresno, CA for RV tires and wheel alignment for any vehicle up to and including 18-wheelers.

http://cf-w.com/

Northern Arizona Tire in Flagstaff and Prescott, AZ have no old tires. The age date on virtually all the tires we saw was within 4-months of manufacture. Jim, the owner, orders tires in small batches and makes sure they are young when they come in, and young when they hit the road.

This company is more than a tire store and can make mechanical repairs on larger vehicles. Their pricing is fair, but they do not deal with extended warranty companies. However, they will give you the necessary documentation to present to your warranty company.

http://www.northaztire.com/

Are there more? Of course, but we haven't used or interviewed other businesses to the extent that we felt confident in a referral. Please feel free to explore for yourself.

Recommended Products:

Exterior Cleaning

Most RV parks and resorts do not allow rig washing in the park. Aero Wash Cosmetics waterless cleaner was designed for washing private airplanes using less than 4-oz. of water. We have used this product for the past several years. It is water based and does an excellent job of cleaning our rig. One 8-oz. bottle will clean our 40-footer twice and the towed vehicle once. The company also offer a concentrate to help with the already reasonable cost.

http://washwax.com/

Toilet Chemicals

Five Star Happy Camper is the best black tank chemicals you can use. It is less expensive than the perfumed chemicals that simply mask the odor from either the black or gray tank. Service technicians have told us that if they have to remove a toilet with a full or an almost full black tank they flush a scoop in the black tank, wait an hour or so and when they remove the toilet there is no odor. Removing tank odors sounds better than smelling perfumed tanks contents.

https://www.5starhappycamper.com/

A word about toilet paper. No, you don't need the high priced single-ply TP. Here's how to test your favorite paper to see if it will work in your rig: Fill a glass quart jar half full of room temperature water. Drop a sheet of your TP into the jar, close and shake. Let it sit for fifteen minutes. If the TP is breaking up and looking more like disolving papier-mâché, you can use it in your holding tanks. To better understand what you are looking for try the same test with a paper towel or face tissue and observe the difference in the two tests.

We have used Costco's TP and Charmin® for years with no problem.

Interior Cleaning

Mild dish soap, baking soda, and vinegar will do all the cleaning of surfaces you will need. Do NOT use harsh chemicals or household toilet bowl cleaners. Any chemicals you put in RV plumbing may damage the valves and gaskets. RV plumbing is not the same as your household plumbing

http://www.pplmotorhomes.com/rvnana/2016/09/always-keep-vinegar-in-your-rv/

CHAPTER 14 / Our List for Purchasing

The following list is what we used when we bought our last motorhome and one, with some modifications, we will use again.

The list is made up of the three categories: want, compromise, and deal-breaker. We start with the outside of the coach and work around, and then the interior, much the way we did the inspections in previous chapters. This list is not the only list, and your wants and deal-breakers will not be the same as ours.

We arrived at our list after looking at hundreds of RVs. We soon realized there is just so much you can do with the long narrow floor space. We encourage you to look at several different manufacturers and classes A, B, or C, as well as towables before you decide. Also look online at the different manufacturer's floor plans. By the time you see the one that fits your needs and lifestyle, you will know it is right for you.

Here is our list (an example):

Exterior Wants

Diesel pusher

40-feet with only two axles

Stay within budget

Through and through basement bays

Side engine radiator

Forward mirrors – both mirrors in front of windshield

Four leveling jacks

Two slides

Two A/C units

Well insulated

No collision damage

Exterior Compromise

Mid-ship door depending on floor plan

HD TV antenna

Box storage bins

Awnings on all windows

Minor stone-chip damage

Interior Wants

Front TV effortlessly cleared when entering or exiting

Light colored interior surfaces

Well anchored overhead cabinets

Large drawers in kitchen, bath, and bedroom

Three burner stove with oven

Large RV refrigerator with icemaker

Adequate lighting for bright interior

Large shower

Closable water closet door

Gas/electric water heater

Dining table and chairs

Queen sized bed

No washer-dryer

No dishwasher

Interior Compromise

Would accept EW bed if step in rear were not too high

Would consider different flooring options

Gas only water heater

Either chairs or couch acceptable in the livingroom

Doors separating different areas, e.g. living to bath, bath to bedroom

Deal-Breakers

Either rear-view mirrors to the side rather than in front

Dark interior

King Bed

Linoleum flooring

Front TV in the way of traffic

Small shower

Low seat commode

Booth dining

Rear radiator on engine

Three leveling jacks instead of four

Gasoline engine

Washing-dryer

Dishwasher

Ceiling Mirrors

No icemaker

What we got

All the exterior wants

All the interior wants

EW bed with small step up

No deal-breakers

CHAPTER 15 / Conclusion

You can get what you want if you are working with the right dealer or private party. We worked with four dealers before finding the one that made it happen.

Some of the dealers were very helpful, letting us know what we could afford, but could not put the deal together. We had challenges, we were self-employed full-time RVers with no fixed residence.

If you lose one deal, don't fret, it wasn't yours, so you didn't lose anything. There will be another just as good or better. Just continue your search.

You do not have to be a mechanic or even a handy person, but you need to prepare for the inevitable breakdown. Be conservative on how hard you press on the fuel pedal and your mileage will be okay. As one RVer told us, his mileage was better than his home, but not as good as his car.

One final word. There is no perfect RV, but there are some that will be livable and comfortable.

Welcome to the exciting and delightful life of RVing! We hope to connect with you on the road.

Jim & Loni Macy

BuyingRVBook@gmail.com

Appendix / Common Weights

Food

Dried Use your shopping list to estimate. Smaller packaging may cost a bit more per ounce, but will probably be easier to pack and store partially used contents. Here are some starters for you:

Spaghetti	1 lb
Crackers	1 lb
Dried Beans	1 lb
Rice	1 lb
Ramen® style soup	3 oz
Mac & Cheese	7.25-9.3 oz*
Stove Top® style Dressing	6 oz*
Cake Mix	18.3 oz*

* indicates an approximation of weight and varies from one producer to another.

Canned and bottles

Can	Wgt.	Diameter	Height
# 1	1-lb	2¾ in.	4 in.
# 2	2-lb	3 7/16 in.	4 9/16 in.
# 3	3-lb	4 3/16 in.	4 7/8 in.
# 6	6-lb		2 X cap of # 3
#10	8-lb	6¼ in.	7 in.

- Don't forget the weight of food in the refrigerator.
- Milk 8-lb/gal

Bottle sizes whether glass plastic or squeeze are so varied there is little point to giving sizes here. Look at what you want to stock and add the estimated weight for a total.

Bedding consists of sheets, pillows, blankets and mattress covers. It depends on the size of the beds you use and the number of beds in your RV. While a queen sheet set may weigh about 51/2 pounds, it will be best to take the bedding you will carry and simply weigh it. A bathroom scale will give a close approximation.

Clothing is another thing you will want to estimate. Sometimes simply hefting the clothes will suffice. You may be surprised at how much your clothing weighs. We would guess that you will probably add 25-30 pounds of clothes per person.

Toiletries including cosmetics, soap, hair products, toothpaste, and other bath necessities can be weighed by using the bathroom scale. Most home scales do not weight within a pounds or so, so round up.

Kitchen equipment may be one of the heavier things you will want along for the ride. Many RVers enjoy the cast iron cookware for outdoor cooking. You will want a secure and stable place for the heavier pots and pans. Don't forget to include the appliances you want such as toaster, coffee-maker and maybe even you food processor. Add in dinnerware and flatware, and you may be surprised at your kitchen's total.

Glossary

Air Bags – A type of suspension as an enhancement to standard springs and shock absorbers. A vehicle may have from two to six bags.

Air Brakes – Typically found on larger vehicles that have a diesel engine.

Basement – The storage found below the living space in an RV. It is usually is accessible from either side of the RV as a through and through storage area.

Batteries – There are three types found in RVs are:

- AGM – The abbreviation for Absorbent Glass Mat which was developed for the military. This is a sealed maintenance free acid battery.
- Flooded – This is a lead battery which is filled with acid. This type needs proper ventilation and maintenance by keeping the fluid level above the plates. Usually refreshed with distilled water.
- Lithium Ion – Has been available for cameras, and other handheld devices. They are now available for an RV's onboard electrical source.

Batteries are divided into two systems, depending on their intended use. The **house** and the **chassis** batteries. This division isolates the chassis battery rather than running it down for household purposes. The Chassis battery will have a large amp draw for starting, and the house batteries will be deep cycle so they can be gradually drawn down to a lower charge level and recharged back to full or nearly full values.

Blackwater – The waste from the toilet(s).

BLM lands – Bureau of Land Management is a Federal Agency that manages Federal land allowing camping in certain areas. Sometimes referred to as Dispersed Camping.

Boondocking – Camping without water, sewer, or electrical hookups. This type of camping is dependent on the self-contained nature of the vehicle.

Coach – Usually used to describe a motorhome or other motorized RV.

Diesel pusher – A diesel engine at the rear of the vehicle.

Dry Camping – See Boondocking.

Engine or Exhaust Brake – A system that uses a diesel engine to enhance braking. This system uses back pressure from damping down the exhaust.

Generator – Supplies 120-volt power to the onboard appliances and usually charges the batteries as well.

Gooseneck – Much like a kingpin, but the receiver fits vertically onto a ball mounted above the rear axle of the tow vehicle.

Gray water – Waste water from everything except the toilet.

Hook-ups – Connections to any of the following

Shore Power provided by sources other than onboard

Water from a water source other than onboard storage

Waste Connection to a sewer system

Cable connection in RV parks or campgrounds.

Inverter – Changes 12-volt battery current into the 120-volt household current. Runs high resistance appliances such as toasters, coffee makers, and microwaves.

King pin – The connecting coupling between a tow vehicle plate and a fifth-wheel. The kingpin is not a gooseneck connector.

Macerator – A machine that grinds up black water solids and pushes them through a small diameter hose.

Membership parks – A park that is for members and member's guests' exclusive use. Qualifying non-members may be allowed to use the facilities on a limited basis. Members always have priority.

PSI – Pounds per Square Inch. A measurement of pressure.

Pusher –Indicating the engine is at the rear of the vehicle.

Rig – A name used to describe an RV or larger vehicle. Can be a travel trailer, fifth-wheel, motorized vehicle, or truck.

Running Gear – Includes the brakes, wheel packings, and tires.

Solar – Collecting electric energy through solar panels which may be attached to the roof of a rig or placed on the ground with connections to the batteries.

Storage bin – The storage found under the living area. May be on both sides of an RV but does not go through from side to side.

Tag axle – An extra axle that is designed to carry extra weight. It is the third axle on a motorhome, but not the second or third axles on a towable.

Tire Scrubbing – Sideways movement as the tire moves around a corner.

Unit – What dealers use to describe vehicles or RVs on their sale's lot. Also used when talking about a group of mixed types of RVs.

Made in the USA
Lexington, KY
30 August 2019